Show-and-Tell
Cycle A Sermons for Lent and Easter

Based on the First Readings of the Revised Common Lectionary

Tony S. Everett

CSS Publishing Co., Inc.
Lima, Ohio

SHOW-AND-TELL

Library of Congress Cataloging-in-Publication Data

Everett, Tony.
   Show-and-tell : and other Cycle A sermons for Lent, Easter ; based on the first readings of the Revised common lectionary / Tony S. Everett. -- 1st ed.
    p. com.
   ISBN 0-7880-2629-1 (alk. paper)
   1. Lent--Sermons. 2. Lenten sermons. 3. Easter--Sermons. 4. Bible. N.T. Acts--Sermons. 5. Bible. O.T.--Sermons. 6. Church year sermons. 7. Common lectionary (1992) I. Title.

BV85.E935 2010
252'.62--dc22

2010040631

ISBN-13: 978-0-7880-2629-4
ISBN-10: 0-7880-2629-1

To Judy
My best friend and life partner

To Lisa, Lori, and Dan
our children and now our colleagues in serving all God's
children

To Sanders, Everett, Finn, Owen, and Isla,
our grandchildren who invite us to see God's good news all
over again for the very first time,
Your love continues as a show-and-tell witness to Jesus.

Acknowledgments

Several people have provided helpful insights and support during the preparation of these reflections on first lesson texts.

Jo Ellen White, Faculty Secretary, has worked with patience, diligence, and excellence in the typing and revising of this manuscript.

Dr. Brian Peterson and Dr. Brent Driggers have supplied welcome focus as I wrestled with the readings from Acts. Their friendship and scholarship are greatly appreciated.

Former parishioners have demonstrated God's presence and guidance during very difficult life circumstances. Their faithful insights and actions truly witness to the living reality of the gospel within every challenge.

The students, alumni, staff, and faculty of Lutheran Theological Southern Seminary continue to show me (and tell me, if I still don't get it) what Jesus is up to in this often complex and confusing life journey.

Acknowledgments

Table of Contents

Introduction

How do you stay awake during a boring sermon? How do you keep from falling asleep during a tediously long-winded lecture? Many of my students and former parishioners (and perhaps some of yours as well) have struggled with these very questions. Some respond by pinching themselves. Others trim their fingernails or compose "to-do" lists. Some try to recall the World Series winners during the entire twentieth century, and still others send text messages or play computer games. Of course, there are a few folks who just can't help themselves. Like Eutychus (one of my all time favorite biblical characters), who had a third floor window seat during one of Paul's lectures and began "to sink off into a deep sleep while Paul talked still longer" (Acts 20:9).

For most of us, it is rather common to see a sleeper or two or ten during our sermons and classes. If we are totally honest, most of us preachers would admit to "pulling a Eutychus" ourselves during a class or sermon at some denominational assembly. Of course, all of us sleepers can blame our snoozing on contextual circumstance such as stress, overwork, sick children, warm temperature, and so forth.

However, there may be another issue involved here. At least part of the problem might be in some commonly held perceptions of the following words: "church members," "worship," and "sermons." As a seminary professor and a frequent interim pastor, I often use these three words as part of a word-association inventory in order to facilitate greater insights and possibilities for ministry. For example, when most people hear the words church members, worship, sermon, what is the first word that they think of?

Although most of those who respond are church members, the phrase "most people" often expanded their frame of reference to include unchurched or "under-churched" acquaintances and family. This admittedly unscientific project is yielding some interesting results. For example, the most frequent word associated with church member is "hypocrite" followed by "believer" and "friend." Worship was associated most often with "boring," "prayer," "singing," and "long." When "sermon" was the focus word, most respondents used phrases instead of one word. Common phrases include "talk about God," "how we should live our lives," "what God wants us to do," and "what the preacher does."

What we expect to receive from worship, sermons, and relationships with other Christians often shapes and limits our thoughts and actions. If we expect worship to be boring and church members to be hypocrites, then they will likely appear that way to us. If we expect sermons to be talks about how God wants us to live (kind of like buying a rider on our fire insurance policy), then it will be more difficult to avoid nodding off in slumber.

Now, Eutychus was literally bored to death. Saint Luke writes that "overcome by sleep, he fell to the ground and was picked up dead" (Acts 20:9). Nobody really knows why Eutychus fell asleep. Was it the midnight hour? The flickering of the many lamps in that upstairs room? The cool breeze from the window? The long lecture by Paul? (Acts 20:7-8) Or something else altogether?

What is known is that when Paul saw this, he stopped his lecture, rushed to the ground floor, held Eutychus in his arms, declared that life was again in him, and then went back upstairs to resume his conversation until dawn.

It seems to me that this small vignette is an excellent model for what show-and-tell witness looks like. Although Paul couldn't prevent Eutychus from falling asleep, he quickly recognized that this was a time to stop telling and start showing what God's restoring love looked like for Paul, for the apostles, and for us. Witness is a matter of show and tell. For many, simply telling people about Jesus can be perceived as boring, moralizing, lecturing, sleep-inducing, and even hypocritical. Likewise, without any explanation, attempts to show the love of Jesus may be perceived as misleading, ambiguous, confusing, manipulating, and even deceiving.

The fact is that communicating God's good news in Jesus Christ includes explanation and demonstration, interpretation, and implementation. Some folks are able to absorb information, gain insight, and even change their behavior simply by following written or oral instructions. Others need a picture of the desired outcome. Still others need to observe a step-by-step demonstration. Many also require another person to walk with them every step of the way.

Learning how to drive an automobile, for example, involves all of these experiences. Passing the written test isn't enough. Listening to a lecture on how to be a good driver is insufficient. Showing the examiner that you have actually practiced the necessary skills is essential. In fact, in the United Kingdom the driving test even requires candidates to "show-and-tell" the examiner various parts of the car engine in order to demonstrate both their knowledge of cars and their driving ability.

In most nursery schools and kindergartens "show-and-tell" is a vital part of the curriculum. Usually a young child will bring an item from home and explain to the class why they chose that specific item, where they got it, and other relevant information. A major purpose of this exercise is to teach children the skills of using speech to communicate the significance of an object or experience.

Unfortunately, many of us mainline Christians have allowed our "tell" to be much more prevalent than our "show." We can talk a lot about our congregation and its programs, but find it difficult to show folks what difference it makes to live within a Christian community. We preachers and professors can talk and write about Jesus but often find it difficult to show what it looks like to be a redeemed child of God.

11

During the seasons of Lent and Easter God shows us clear pictures of a new reality in the good news of Jesus Christ. From ashes to a wooden cross and from the empty tomb to the ascension we catch a glimpse of what God's love looks like. First lesson texts are filled with images inviting us to participate in an unfolding journey that weaves us into a brand new and eternal community. Throughout Lent God shows us images of locusts (Joel 2) and recipes (Exodus 12), a teacher's tongue (Isaiah 50) and a suffering servant (Isaiah 52), dry bones (Ezekiel 37) and a sly serpent (Genesis 2), water from a rock (Exodus 17), an elderly couple's impossible mission (Genesis 12), and a secret king-making ceremony (1 Samuel 16).

During the season of Easter our first lesson texts are from the book of Acts. Here the author communicates the good news by showing through events and story rather than by telling through letter and lecture. Peter's speeches explain the significance of amazing events (Acts 2 and 10). Paul illustrates what a culturally sensitive and faithful witness looks like (Acts 17). The martyrdom of Stephen demonstrates that the power of the ascended Lord overcomes the control of the world every time (Acts 7). The last earthly words of Jesus and his ascension show and tell the primary mission of the church (Acts 1).

The sermons in this volume are actually reflections on specific biblical texts assigned to be read during the seasons of Lent and Easter. The context in which they were written (a seminary professor's desk in South Carolina during the 2008-2009 academic year) is certainly not the same as the setting in which you are reading them. Some of you may prefer to study these texts and reflections by yourselves. Others may choose to include them as part of a Sunday school class or weekly Bible study group.

However, as you wrestle with these first lesson texts, I encourage you to begin in prayer with an openness to receive the good news God is showing you in each passage. What does this look like in your own life? What does this look like in your parish? What are some congregational blind spots and unanswered questions; factors that inhibit seeing what God might be showing you? What are some witness opportunities that emerge within this scripture? What are some particular demonstrations of witness that are already happening in your parish? However you engage these scripture lessons, allow the Holy Spirit to show you again and again the reality of God's good news so that you may show-and-tell it with excitement and passion.

— Tony S. Everett

Locusts Happen

It was never this bad; not in their lifetime, not in anybody's lifetime. It was so terrible that children would tell their children who would then tell their children about this time of thick clouds, darkness, and destruction. All the fields were devastated and the grain was ruined. Herds of cattle and sheep were dying of starvation. Fruit-bearing trees were splintered and drying up, withering away like the people's joy. It seemed like the whole world was coming to a terrible end. Everyone was lamenting and mourning. Everything seemed out of control.

What was going on here? A military invasion? The results of a nuclear blast? A plague? Well, yes and no. This is the setting for today's scripture text, described in the first chapter of Joel. It was an invading army of locusts — common enough in Old Testament times — but this may have been the worst ever — maybe even as bad as the locust horde that God visited upon Egypt as the eighth of ten Exodus "plague persuaders" (Exodus 10:3-20).

Nothing seemed able to stop the locust onslaught. Each locust seemed larger than life to an overwhelmed people. "Its teeth are lion's teeth and it has the fangs of a lioness" (Joel 1:6). Thousands, probably millions of these creatures blackened the sky and devoured almost everything in sight. It was hopeless, helpless misery. Locusts happen!

What the cutting locust left, the swarming locust has eaten. What the swarming locust left, the hopping locust has eaten, and what the hopping locust left, the destroying locust has eaten.

— Joel 1:4

15

Locusts happen! Now we can understand the alarm Joel calls for. Now we can see what Joel means by clouds and thick darkness crawling closer and spreading everywhere. Nothing has ever been this bad before. Nothing will ever be this bad again (2:2). Locusts happen! Where could the people turn when there was nowhere to turn?

Where are the locusts in your life on this Ash Wednesday? What seems to be chaotic and out of control? Where are those fragile and tender places in your hearts? For some, financial burdens have become as devastating as a horde of locusts. For others, family crises fill every thought and dream just like swarming locusts. Persisting sorrow and grief can drain energy reserves just like the cutting locusts slice through strong grape vines in the most fertile vineyard. Locusts happen! Where can you turn when there is nowhere to turn?

It was Shrove Tuesday, the day before Ash Wednesday. It was a time to prepare for Lent with a youth-sponsored pancake supper and an outdoor worship service that featured the burning of palm fronds from last year's Palm Sunday in order to make ashes that would be used in tomorrow's Ash Wednesday service.

Everything was in order and the people were gathered around a charcoal grill in the church parking lot. Dried palm fronds were in the grill. The lector began reading from Psalm 80:3-8.

You turn us back to dust and say, "Turn back, you mortals... for we are consumed by your anger; by your wrath we are over-whelmed."

Meanwhile, Pastor Andy was unable to light the palms — so he poured on more charcoal lighter; then more and more, and... WHOOSH! Flames shot up from the grill into overhanging branches of an apple tree... from which they

16

spread into another and still another fruit tree. Fortunately, firefighters arrived quickly and extinguished the blaze with minimal damage and no injuries... except to Pastor Andy's pride, that is. From that day on throughout his ministry, Pastor Andy's Shrove Tuesday "show and tell" became a living memory in that congregation's story... a story "like has never been from of old nor will be again... for ages to come" (Joel 2:3). Locusts happen!

Where do you turn when there's nowhere to turn? Where do you turn when locusts happen? Who can extinguish the pain in your hearts that just won't go away? Who can rewrite the story of your own shame and failure? Who can stop the locusts from crawling into every corner of your soul? Where do you turn when your best efforts turn into an all-consuming mess?

When everything that can go wrong is going wrong for God's people in our text and for God's people on this Ash Wednesday, Joel proclaims God's message:

> *Yes even now, says the Lord; return to me with all your heart, with fasting, with weeping, and with mourning; rend your hearts and not your clothing.*
> — Joel 2:12-13

So... where do we turn when there's nowhere to turn? To the Lord. How do we do this? Most Christians are taught to do this through Lenten spiritual disciplines of prayer, fasting, mourning, and meditating. Isn't that what Lent is all about? A time for renewing faith through spiritual discipline... time sort of like spring training for professional baseball or spring practice for college football. Doesn't the word "Lent" actually have its origin in the Anglo Saxon word meaning "springtime"? Isn't Lent like spring training for people who want to learn how to cope with or even avoid all problems of life? Hmm...

17

Wouldn't it be wonderful if resolving problems in life could be handled by a little spiritual coaching during spring break? How great would it be if getting rid of life's locusts were as easy as following the dots in a child's puzzle book? Don't you wish your life was more like a movie or television program in which the good always wins in the end? Every story should have a happy ending. Every life should be filled with joyous music and dancing. Every cloud should have a silver lining. Every sour lemon that comes our way should be squeezed into lemonade by a couple of spiritual disciplines. Right?

Well, sadly, it isn't that simplistic. Trumpet blowing, lamenting, fasting, and garment tearing did not drive away every locust horde in Old Testament times. Outward acts of piety were not necessarily guarantors of faithful relationships with the Lord... not then, not now. Our best efforts and intentions often fail. Evil exists. Locust happens!

So where do we turn when there is nowhere to turn?

Well, obviously, to the Lord. Not because the Lord guarantees to make the locusts disappear forever; not because the Lord promises that we will never be ashamed or sad or guilty again. So, why bother to return to the Lord anyway? We can turn to the Lord because the Lord has already turned toward us.

Here is Joel's answer... "for he is gracious and merciful, slow to anger, and abounding in steadfast love" (Joel 2:13). In the midst of life's overwhelming locust swarms, the overflowing love of the Lord comforts and strengthens us for the daily journey. The ashes of shame placed on our foreheads today reveal the cross of victory that God has placed into our hearts. In Jesus Christ, the cross of ashes placed on our foreheads today will disappear in a little while. Nevertheless, the water poured and the cross made on our foreheads at baptism are marks of God's steadfast and forever love. The cross of ashes on our foreheads today will disappear soon. The body

18

and blood of the crucified Christ will strengthen our hearts forever. Amen.

Lent 1
Genesis 2:15-17; 3:1-7

Will this Be on the Test?

What do you think might be the most common questions teachers in all grade levels hear from their students? You are correct if you were thinking of something to do with passing examinations. Will this be on the test? What do we have to know to pass the test? What happens if we fail? Do we get another chance?

Beginning soon after birth (some folks might say soon after conception) children are measured and compared to arbitrary standards of physical, mental, social, and even emotional well being. Parents and grandparents share pictures and compare achievements. Physicians measure and chart. Professional educators establish entrance specifications and performance expectations. As we progress through life, measurements of what we know and how we grow determine how others relate to us as well as how we view ourselves.

For many, "Will it be on the test?" can easily become the most important question in life. Success and failure are determined by demonstrated performance scores. In many states, schools and teachers themselves are also evaluated by scores made by students on standardized tests.

So, this situation results in an even more challenging question for everyone... students and teachers, school boards and communities; should teachers prepare students to master specific skills and information needed to pass a particular test or should they prepare their classes with more general problem-solving skills and information that will help them pass tests of successful living in the midst of all sorts of life challenges? Of course there is no easy answer.

Both methods of preparation are needed for growth and maturity in life. As you know well, life is a series of one test after another; written and oral, multiple choice and true-false, essay and demonstration.

The way we learn to prepare for and take tests really does shape the way we adapt and cope with life challenges at work and school, in our family and neighborhood, in our nation and world, and even in our congregation.

Hopefully, we have learned how to prepare for and to take tests... not in order to simply survive but to really thrive in the process. Ideally, we have learned that passing one test prepares us to pass the next. However, sadly enough, we often repeat the same preparation mistakes. We wind up barely hanging on, scarcely surviving in an "almost but-not-quite" life.

The season of Lent is a season of preparation for participation in the crucifixion and resurrection of Jesus Christ. For many Christians this preparation includes a six week discipline of giving up things such as sugary sweets and salty snacks, watching television, or listening to popular music. Others prepare by placing a coin or dollar bill into a self-denial folder each day. We do these things during Lent to remind us of what Jesus gave up for us and how much Jesus sacrificed for us. And then when Lent is over, on Easter evening, we gorge ourselves on chocolate Easter eggs and salted peanuts while the television competes with iPods for our attention.

We prepared for the test all right. We experienced Christ's death for us, and we survived. However, we did not prepare for Christ's continuing life in us. We did not prepare for Christ's daily dying and rising with us. This Lenten preparation includes learning and practicing spiritual disciplines that will continue beyond the Lenten season; a preparation for an ongoing and renewing relationship that Christ initiated through his dying and rising. So, we are not total failures.

We have this preparation thing partly correct, but we only see part of the whole picture.

Now, let's look at our text in Genesis. Here Eve and Adam only paid attention to one aspect of the five gifts of life God had given them. First, God gave them a beautiful garden setting in which to live. Second, God gave them the freedom to wander around and to share in the garden's abundance. Third, God gave Adam and Eve the gift of each other... the gift of human relationship. Fourth, God gave them a specific and very limited command of obedience; eat anything you want here, but if you eat from the tree of knowledge of good and evil, you will die. And, God's fifth and final gift to Adam and Eve in our text is a gift of vocation that brings meaning and purpose to life... caring for God's garden.

Hey, Adam and Eve! Listen up now! This will be on the test. In fact here is the actual question: Describe the five gifts God has given you and then present a "show-and-tell" demonstration of how you balance these in daily life. Well, we all know that Adam and Eve failed miserably. They ignored four gifts and concentrated on only one: obedience to God's command prohibiting them from eating a specific kind of fruit.

Sadly it is all too easy for us to look at today's text with the narrow focus of Adam and Eve. What does God forbid us from doing? We tend to emphasize this much more frequently than what God permits or encourages us to do.

Don was preparing to attend Sunday worship with his fiancée Lorna and her family. Since it was his very first time in that parish and not wanting to embarrass himself in front of Lorna's family by saying or doing "the wrong thing," Don asked Lorna to review what would be expected during the service. Lorna and her parents carefully explained liturgical actions such as kneeling and blessing, signing the cross and singing the psalmody.

All went smoothly until the brief time for quiet reflection following the pastor's sermon. Suddenly Lorna sneezed, quite loudly. Immediately she whispered to Don, "Bless me."

Desperately, Don tried to remember what he had just been taught about blessings in church. Nothing came to mind. He started to perspire, knowing that he was about to humiliate himself in front of his financée and most of her family and friends.

Again, this time with more volume, Lorna asked, "Don, aren't you going to bless me?"

Wanting to do things right and still not wanting to offend anyone, Don blurted out, "I can't bless you because I don't know how!"

Poor Don. Exclusive focus on avoiding the wrong often results in forgetting to do what is right. Primary concentration on what is prohibited tends to minimize gifts that are to be celebrated.

On the one hand, like Don, we pay so much attention to these things in order to escape humiliation. On the other hand, we focus so much on what God forbids, well, just because it is forbidden. For example, God's gifts to Adam and Eve were wonderful. Who among us could really complain about receiving a beautiful place to live, delicious food, a life partner, a trusted relationship with God, a purpose for living, and the freedom to enjoy it all?

Sure, trust, vocation, relationships, and freedom are pretty good ideas… but, hey, what is forbidden might really feel great. It can't hurt to find out more, can it?

And thus it begins. As you know very well… when you really want something, you will listen to everything, convince yourself of anything, and wind up with exactly nothing. The serpent made this happen quickly. Do you see how it ignores four of God's gifts and quickly asks what God has forbidden? Eve answers specifically and correctly, but the serpent's seductive trap is sprung. The serpent twists obedience into a barrier to avoid and an option from which to choose. For Adam and Eve, the immediate result of obtaining the very thing that God prohibited was much more appealing than enduring the daily challenge of balancing all five gifts that God had given. They tasted the fruit, failed their test, and fell flat on their faces. We also taste, fail, and fall; forever captive to sin and unable to free ourselves. When we really want something, there's always a serpent around to convince us to do anything so that we wind up with nothing again and again. Forever failures.

Lent is a season for preparing for a test, all right. However, the test isn't ours to take. It is ours to celebrate Jesus Christ who has already taken and passed it with triumphant honors. Our preparation time this Lent is one of paying attention to God's show-and-tell lessons of a cross, a loving splash of forgiveness, a nourishing taste of God's presence, and a living Word of God's promise for our lives... test taken, test passed! Given and shed for you. Amen.

Voice in a Vacuum

At first reading it seems as if today's text is all about Abram's journey from relative obscurity to universal fame; from being a childless husband in a tiny and insignificant family to becoming the founding father of a great multitude of nations. Now what would it look like if we read this story with God as the main character? What would it look like if we examined the text from the perspective of God's initiating action instead of Abram's immediate faithful response? After all, it's pretty intimidating to try to compare our own somewhat tenuous faith to the unquestioning faithfulness of a religious superhero.

Let's look at what God does for Abram and really for us as well. God enters an aging, aimless, and barren existence; one whose pattern seems set; whose future is inevitably established. God's people had been trapped in an incredible "same old, same old" reality from one generation after another, ever since the Lord confounded people's languages and scattered them throughout the earth following that tower of Babel debacle (Genesis 11). Barren and empty; meaningless and without direction... like being trapped in a vacuum. Have you ever felt like that?

Here's a story that some of you may have heard before. It happened in a high school physics class one cold and damp March morning. Mr. Jones was explaining that a vacuum was a space in which all matter and even most of the existing air has been removed. During his lecture, Mr. Jones noticed Bob and Bill talking animatedly in the back row.

"Gentlemen," he said in a stern voice, "I'm assuming that you are in the middle of a lively debate about the properties of a vacuum instead of arguing about the upcoming NCAA Basketball Tournament brackets. Am I right?"

"Ah, yes, of course," Bob replied. "You bet," echoed Bill.

"Well, then," Mr. Jones responded. "Let me ask you an easy question. If you were in a vacuum and I was speaking to you, would you be able to hear my voice?"

"Uh, that depends, I guess," Bob stammered. "Yeah, it depends all right," Bill added.

"Okay, go on. It depends on what?" asked Mr. Jones, hoping against hope that Bob and Bill had at least paid some attention to the part of the lecture that described how sound waves travel through air.

No such luck, Mr. Jones. Together Bob and Bill proclaimed, "It depends on whether or not the vacuum is on or off."

Hmmm... The class laughed. Mr. Jones sighed. Bob and Bill left for the principal's office.

Indeed, it is hard to hear any voice, especially God's voice, in a vacuum. That's true if you are thinking of a life space barren of outside stimulation; devoid of personal and communal vitality and hope. It's also true if you are thinking of a life space full of noise and clutter, chaos and confusion.

What does your life space look like... in your family? Your community? Your congregation? In your own soul? Are you overwhelmed by the chaos? Bored to tears by endless monotony? Exhausted in helplessness? Abandoned by those close to you? Does it seem like all your energy is being sucked into a vast black hole from which there is no escape and nothing can penetrate?

This is where God enters and God's voice permeates the deepest vacuum of the soul. Abram did nothing special to make this happen. God's voice spoke to him anyway. Neither can we do anything special to compel God to enter our lives and speak to us. God just speaks anyway.

To Abram and to us God speaks both words of promise and of mission. Many Christians remember the mission: "Go! Move out and move on! Don't even think about where you're going. I'll tell you later!" (Genesis 12:1). Now, that's a pretty scary mission; one so challenging that most of us hope God never speaks to us like that. Better to live in a vacuum you know than start on a mission you don't know. After all, we are not now and never will be religious superstars like Abram.

Nevertheless, God enters the vacuum spaces of our lives and speaks words of promise and purpose. Look again at our text. God's promise (Genesis 12:2-3) comes before Abram does anything or goes anywhere (Genesis 12:4). God gives the mission and provides the promised blessing to complete it. God's blessing here does not simply mean God's approval. The gift of God's blessing is also a gift of God's power.

Pay attention to the words of God's promises here. "I will show you; I will make of you a great nation; I will bless you... so that you will be a blessing and in you all the families of the earth shall be blessed" (Genesis 12:1-3). God gave Abram a mission and the promised power to complete it. Through Abram God created a new future and a new community that continues to be a blessing to all families of the earth. Remember that the promise of God's blessing is also the same thing as the promise of God's power.

So, what does this mean for us? The new future is now. The new community is the Church. God's promised blessing to Abram is alive within us today. The real power of God's promise swells within each Christian and each congregation.

Too many Christians may still be living in a "same old same old" vacuum; immobilized by overwhelming stress and barren of hope for renewal. Too many Christians may be forgetting that God's power is the essential ingredient in God's blessing. Too many Christians may still be thinking that "God bless you" only means "God approves of you, but hasn't given you any power to make a difference in your lives or in your communities." God just approves/blesses our living trapped in a fragile and self-defeating vacuum. God doesn't give us any power to do anything about it.

Not long ago, near Seattle, Washington, a baby whale and its mother were discovered in a river several miles inland from the Pacific Ocean. The huge creatures appeared to be lost. Many rescue efforts seemed to confuse the whales even more and only drove them farther away from the ocean. Finally, rescuers lowered speakers and played whale sounds into the water. The trapped creatures began to grow calmer and soon followed the familiar sounds back home into the vast Pacific Ocean.

What does God's promise sound like to you? What does God's blessing look like for you? What does God's power feel like for you?

Today, the Second Sunday of Lent, God chooses to enter your life, no matter how empty it may seem or how lost you may feel. Today God shows you a forever promise in the baptismal font. Today God gives you words of blessing from the altar table, "Given and shed for you." Today God gives you power for mission, to be a blessing to others.

So what does it look like to "be a blessing"?

Here are some examples discovered in just one day by listening to parishioners and reading the newspaper. Standing in a long grocery store checkout line, a woman was startled when the man behind her handed her an envelope and inside was a $50 bill attached to a note simply saying, "Take it if you need it. Pass it on." What was astounding here was not just that the envelope was passed forward, but that many people added more dollars.

Another man described a similar situation while he was in a long line of automobiles moving slowly toward a toll booth at a long bridge. When he finally arrived to pay his fee, the official in the booth said that his toll had been paid by someone in the car ahead. You can guess what happened next. The man paid the toll for the next automobile and so on.

When Sam returned from a youth mission trip into a hurricane ravaged area, he organized monthly "mini-mission" trips into his local community. When Mary's twelve-year-old daughter received a kidney transplant donated by a stranger, Mary developed an organ donation advocacy ministry in her local conference of churches. When Thomas had a birthday party, he asked that all gifts be soccer balls and equipment that he could donate to his congregation's missionary in East Africa. When his brother Stephen celebrated his birthday, he donated his gifts to the local chapter of Big Brothers and Big Sisters.

What does it look like to be a blessing?

Look around a bit. You will see examples everywhere. Watch what happens with the folks who observe these often small acts of kindness. Watch for the smiles, the sighs, the changes in facial expressions and body postures. Being a blessing often shows God's power and love. Being a blessing brings a contagious excitement and purpose into the empty spaces of life.

Pay attention here. Abram does not just hang around the campfire with old friends and relatives waiting for folks to come to him to get a blessing. Because he received God's promise and power, he set off on God's mission to pull up stakes and go to an unknown destination of desert spaces: parched lands, frozen hearts, and false promises. Abram met with people who didn't look like him, didn't think like him, didn't speak like him; people who were broken, fragile, empty, oppressed, searching.

Hey, that sounds a lot like us. And Abram's mission sounds like it might be ours too. But how can we do that really? How can we ever be a blessing to others when we are struggling in our own vacuum with our own problems?

Oh yeah, that's right. We can't do this alone. Neither could Abram. God gave Abram promise, purpose, and power. He received a blessing so that he could be a blessing.

Today God gives us the blessing of promise and power in Jesus Christ and sends us to be God's blessing in the vacuum of others' lives. Amen.

Is the Lord Among Us or Not?

When most folks first come to seminary they enter with very high expectations of participating in a grand and glorious spiritual high. No doubts. No despair. Just higher and higher peaks of power and wonder. No valleys. No problems. Life together should be like belonging to a fabulous family filled with good feelings. No murmuring. No quarreling. Just happiness. Most students and their accompanying families have left behind real jobs that paid real money. They have left homes, friends, and relatives. They have left caring, supporting, compassionate congregations. Something old and familiar has ended. Now they are expecting something new and fabulous to begin. The last thing they expected was to find themselves wandering in an uncomfortable and confusing wilderness filled with more questions than answers. Is the Lord among us or not? Tell us! Show us right now!

When people first join a congregation many enter with similar expectations. They anticipate becoming part of a stable, intimate, continually joy-filled community. At least two-thirds of new parishioners have experienced significant life changes during the previous year. These include changes in location, occupation, family situation, income, school, friends, neighborhood, and congregation. The familiar has ended. Wilderness wandering has begun. The last thing they expect from their new congregations is more confusion and discomfort. No wilderness! No way! Please! Not now! Is the Lord among us or not? Tell us! Show us! Right now!

Well, we all know from our own experience that throughout history God's people have faced times of pain and doubt, broken dreams and unmet expectations, times of internal bickering and external fights, and times when their leaders and even their God seemed to be incompetent and untrustworthy. We have all experienced times when the freely flowing waters in our hearts seemed to become buried by the dry dust of our sins… times when we too have questioned: Is the Lord among us or not? Tell us! Show us! Right now!

In today's text, an enslaved Hebrew people had left their comfortable routines and the familiar food and shelter in Egypt with a grand, glorious, miraculous march through the sea. Onward to freedom! Onward to the promised land flowing with milk and honey! Onward following the Lord and his servant Moses with a pillar of cloud by day and a pillar of fire by night (Exodus 13:21). Onward in a state of awesome spiritual wonder! No more problems! No more slavery! We'll be in the promised land before you know it! God is with us and all is right in our world!

However, in reality, the journey was anything but quick and easy. It was full of continued, aimless, and endless wandering within a hostile and barren wilderness. Their food was not the familiar meat and vegetables flavored with Egyptian spices. Their wilderness food was a flaky residue left over from nightly insect activity on the leaves of plants. This new food was called, "What is it?" or in Hebrew "manna" (Exodus 16:14). When they weren't gathering manna, they were looking for water. When they weren't reminiscing about the good times they enjoyed back in Egypt, they were complaining to the Lord and blaming Moses about the miserable times they were experiencing here in the wilderness.

For example, even before they left Egypt, the Hebrew slaves blamed Moses when Pharaoh forced them to make bricks without straw (Exodus 5:15-20). Then when they saw the Egyptians pursuing them, the Hebrews complained and blamed Moses for bringing them out of Egypt. You can almost hear their whining "I-told-you-so."

What have you done to us bringing us out of Egypt? Is this not the very thing we told you in Egypt, "Let us alone and let us serve the Egyptians?" For it would have been better for us to serve the Egyptians than to die in the wilderness.

— Exodus 14:11-12

Then, right after the Lord provided a miraculous escape by parting the waters of the sea, the Hebrews complained about the food.

If only we had died by the hand of the Lord in the land of Egypt where we sat by the fleshpots and ate our fill of bread; for you have brought us out into the wilderness to kill this whole assembly with hunger.

— Exodus 16:2-3

Wilderness journeys aren't for sissies. They are tough. Moving from one way of life to another is always filled with unexpected obstacles and difficult challenges. No matter how wonderful the destination is; no matter how clearly the promised vision is described, getting there is tougher than expected. The more difficult and distant the destination seems, the easier it is to be diverted and discouraged along the way. The more remote the future dream appears, the easier it is to focus only on the discomforts of the present and to yearn for the pleasures of the past. Is the Lord among us or not? Tell us! Show us! Right now!

In our text today, the folks had had enough... again. They were thirsty... again. They complained to Moses... again. "Why did you bring us out of Egypt to kill us and our children and our livestock with thirst?" (Exodus 17:3). In Numbers 20:5 they called their present location a "wretched place... no place for grain, or figs, or vines, or pomegranates" like they had back in Egypt.

Finally a frustrated Moses cried out to the Lord: "What shall I do with this people? They are almost ready to stone me" (Exodus 17:4).

Here are God's people — God's chosen people — in the wilderness murmuring and moaning, complaining and blaming, quarreling and testing. Can you believe this ungrateful behavior after all that God had done for them? After all that God is still doing for them? After all that God has promised them?

Before we evaluate their wilderness behavior too harshly, consider what it's like for you in your own wilderness. What is it like to be discouraged and depressed? What is it like to have a dream dashed to pieces on the rocks of disappointment? What is it like to have your hopes raised high only to plummet into the depths of despair? To be misunderstood by friends and family? To be blamed for something you didn't do by your teacher at school or your boss at work? Does it ever seem like no matter how hard you try to adjust to a new situation the same problems arise and the same mistakes persist? How do you handle times of doubt and drought, spiritual dryness and thirst? How do you cope with the complaints of other wilderness travelers and being blamed then for their own dusty spirits and depleted energy? Is the Lord in your place or not?

Pay careful attention here. God did not give Moses a website full of effective methods for managing conflict. Neither did God provide Moses with a list of snappy replies that will stifle complaining and eliminate blaming. Instead, God gave Moses directions for how to find water.

Where's the water supply in your wilderness right now? What guidance is God giving to you? Look again at the fifth and sixth verses in our text. Here God's guidance to Moses and to you are similar. Go for a walk with some wise and trusted Christian elders. Bring with you a sign, a memory, a symbol of how God's presence was your guide through previous difficulties. And when you do this, God tells both Moses and you, "I will be standing there in front of you."

It is in these dry wilderness times that God leads us to see flowing water. God leads us to the solid rock of ages, Jesus Christ, from whom all blessings flow. God stands in front of us at the baptismal font reminding us of God's own life-giving, life-changing love that leads us through any wilderness with a love that never lets us go thirsty.

Here in your congregation and in your own lives there will be wilderness times of doubting and despairing, complaining and blaming, moaning and murmuring, grumbling and groaning. That's normal. That's even biblical. As the Hebrews did, you will often lose sight of God's presence with you and God's promise to you and for you. You will search desperately for a quick fix for your most recent and troublesome problems.

That too is normal and biblical. In fact, Moses even gave names to the very place where this happened. He called the place Massah [test] and Meribah [quarreling] because the Israelites quarreled and tested the Lord saying, "Is the Lord in this place or not?" (Exodus 17:7).

So, is the Lord in this place, your place, or not? If people bicker and blame does that mean God is not there? If there is pain and despair, hunger and thirst, does that mean that God is absent? If there is violence and oppression or disease and depression does that mean that God does not care?

Is the Lord in this place or not?

Yes, indeed. The Lord is in this place, all right! The Lord Jesus entered the dark abyss of the world. He suffered, bled, and died in this world for you and for all human kind. Where bodies are broken, Christ is there. Where blood is poured out, Christ is there. Where souls are splashed with flowing water, Christ is there. Where God's word is spoken, Christ is there. Where God's people gather, Christ is there.

Is the Lord in this place or not? Look around. God is showing you. Listen up, God is telling you. And all God's people say, "Amen!"

Hey, What's that Sound?

Here's a familiar story. Two large oak trees had fallen across Bob's front lawn during a huge thunderstorm the previous evening. Deciding to cut them up for firewood, Bob went to the local hardware store to purchase a chain saw.

"I need the best chain saw you have," Bob told the store manager.

"Yes sir," said the manager. "This one here will cut up to ten cords of wood in an eight-hour work day."

"I'll take it," Bob replied, "I need to get those trees off my lawn and turn them into fireplace fuel for next winter."

As Bob was leaving the hardware store with his new purchase, the manager reminded him, "Remember, be sure to keep it filled with the right mix of oil and gasoline."

"I know, I know all that," Bob responded, in a hurry to get home and start cutting wood.

"And don't forget to oil the chain every half-hour or so," added the manager who could tell that perhaps Bob had little if any previous chain saw experience.

With his hand on the exit door Bob sighed heavily and with an impatient voice, dripping with sarcasm, retorted, "Look, I'm in a hurry to get the job done. I can figure this out for myself. I'm not stupid."

"Hmmm…" thought the manger to herself.

So, Bob worked all day, faithfully oiling the chain every half hour. By suppertime Bob was hot, dusty, and exhausted. Sadly, he had been able to cut only one quarter of one cord of wood… certainly not close to the ten cords mentioned by the hardware store manger. "Tomorrow is another day," Bob thought. "I'll make up for lost time then."

Well, the next day was an instant replay of the first. Bob oiled the chain every thirty minutes, just like he was told, but he still ended the day aching, frustrated, and fatigued, with only a few pieces of cut and stacked wood to show for it. "This is ridiculous," Bob murmured to himself. "First thing in the morning I'm going to show up at the hardware store with my chain saw and get to the bottom of this. I'll demand that the manager either fix my saw, give me a new one, or return my money."

At the hardware store the following morning Bob confronted the manager. He dropped the chain saw at her feet and exclaimed, "You told me this thing would cut up to ten cords of wood a day. Well, I've worked myself to the bone with this saw for two days and it hasn't even cut one cord. What are you going to do about it?" Bob exclaimed defiantly.

"Let's take a look," said the manage keeping her voice calm. "Are you sure you kept oiling the chain?"

Growing more and more exasperated, Bob snapped, "Of course I did. I oiled the chain every half hour. You could set your watch by my chain oiling. I wake up at night every thirty minutes, thinking that its time to oil the chain. I'm exhausted I tell you. I did what you told me. This saw is broken. Something's wrong with it! You have to…"

Interrupting Bob's diatribe, the store manager said, "Let's see what the problem is." She grasped the handle of the chain saw with her left hand and jerked the handle of the cord on top of the motor with her right hand and suddenly a loud "brr" fills the hardware store.

"Hey, what's that sound?" asked Bob, timidly.

Like Bob, it's possible to go through life with our own repeated and frustrated attempts at success. Like Bob, it's possible to find ourselves exhausted and miserable at the end of each day with little or nothing to show for our efforts. Like Bob, we often have opinions that are so tightly held that they keep us from seeing the obvious source of power in front of us. Like Bob, we can easily overlook new possibilities and waste enormous energy by endlessly repeating the same mistakes.

Today's Old Testament text is a story of discerning God's power and presence. Where do we find it? How do we get it? What do we do with it?

In today's lesson we learn that Saul's kingship in Israel is near its end. Saul has disobeyed the Lord (1 Samuel 15) who then tells Samuel, "I have rejected him from being king over Israel" (1 Samuel 16:1). Then the Lord sent Samuel on a strange mission that concluded with the anointing of David as the next king. Now pay attention. As you read this text, notice that the main character is the Lord. The critical decisions are made by the Lord. The mission directions are given by the Lord. Samuel, Jessie, and his sons, and especially David, are mere actors in a story that the Lord produces, directs, and plays the lead role. David doesn't say a word. He simply shows up.

Now, where is God's power? God knows where and sends Samuel there (1 Samuel 16:1). God's power, like the chain saw power cord for Bob, is in surprising and easily overlooked places and people. God sent Samuel south to Judah to "Jesse, the Bethlehemite and his sons. God had already selected one of them to be king" (1 Samuel 16:1).

Now, what does this tell us about where God's power and presence can be discovered? Saul was from the north and the tribe of Benjamin. Samuel was much more familiar with the northern context, and expressed his fear of ever going to Bethlehem. So, the first place we know God's power is located is in the new, the unfamiliar, even the scary places and people... people and places that are easily overlooked and appear to be the least likely to be chosen by God.

41

After demonstrating his peaceful intentions, Samuel invited Jesse and his sons to worship with him in the local sanctuary. Samuel looked at each of Jesse's sons, noticing stature, strength, and handsome appearance. An impressive looking group all right. Surely, the Lord had chosen one of these strapping fellows to be the next king of all Israel. But the Lord rejected all seven, telling Samuel, "The Lord does not see as mortals see; they look on outward appearance, but the Lord looks on the heart" (1 Samuel 16:7).

In other words, don't rely on first impressions. What you see on the outside does not always indicate what is on the inside of a person. We've all heard phrases that describe folks whose outward appearance displays competence and confidence, but upon closer examination demonstrate uselessness and instability. Some that come to mind include the following: "Her porch light's on but nobody at home." "His elevator doesn't make it to the top floor." You might know a few more.

Wilma, 20th of 22 children, suffered from polio as a very young child. By age six, Wilma had also survived double pneumonia, scarlet fever, and whooping cough. She was frail and weak, often needing assistance to accomplish even the smallest tasks at home or school. Based only on her outward appearance, Wilma was destined for a life of poverty, dependence, and frustration. However, Wilma had a fierce determination to overcome this crippling illness.

Through grueling exercises and relentless discipline, Wilma not only began to walk, she started to run. Then Wilma not only ran, she ran fast, faster than anyone in her school. The little girl with frail legs and a fragile body had become a young woman with a powerful body and a courageous heart.

At the 1960 Olympics in Rome, Wilma Rudolph didn't just run, she sprinted her way to three Olympic gold medals:

for the 100 and 200 meter dashes and as anchor in the 400 meter relay.

"The Lord does not see what mortals see… the Lord looks on the heart" (1 Samuel 16:7).

So, where is the Lord's power and presence located? The Lord knew where and sent Samuel there in today's text. The Lord knows where and sends you there in your own life journey.

First, scripture reminds us that God's power is in new, risky, even scary places. Samuel went, although with some fear (1 Samuel 16:2) to the unfamiliar and potentially perilous southern regions near Bethlehem in order to meet with unknown strangers and anoint one of them as king when Israel already had a king. Now that's pretty worrisome, if not downright dangerous. And yet, the Lord was there and had already planned for Israel's future to emerge from this very encounter.

Second, our scripture lesson reminds us that the Lord's presence and power are deep inside our own hearts. Few, if any of us, will become great world leaders like David or Olympic champions like Wilma Rudolph. Nevertheless, it is the Lord's power within us that prepares us to enter the new and challenging spaces that lie just before us.

So, what do we do to get the Lord's presence and power anyway? Well, nothing, really. We don't do anything to "get it." God gives it to us! Look again at today's lesson. David didn't say anything at all. In fact, he didn't even do anything except show up, "and the Spirit of the Lord came mightily upon David from that day forward" (1 Samuel 16:13).

The Lord gave power and presence to us and for us on the cross. The Lord gave that power and presence to us and for us in the water of baptism, in the bread and wine of Holy Communion, in the living word of scripture, and in the gathering of the Lord's people. The Lord has promised to continue giving forever. How do we get this gift again? Like David in our lesson, just show up! God has given, is giving, and has promised to continue to give God's own spirit of power and presence forever.

And finally, what do we do with this gift when we get it? Just like Samuel in today's scripture, God will show us what to do, give you instructions on how to do it, and send you where it must be done.

Brrr… what's that sound, anyway? That's the power and presence of the Lord Jesus Christ filling our heart. That's the wind of the spirit of the Lord inviting you to become part of an exciting and soul-filling adventure. Amen.

Lent 5
Ezekiel 37:1-14

A Breath of Fresh Air

This story has been shared at many church gatherings recently. Three parish deacons were hiking across an old wooden foot bridge fifty feet above a dry and rocky creek bed. They stopped for a moment to absorb the breath-taking view of distant hillsides, green pastures filled with grazing cattle, and endless rows of tall cornstalks waving in the gentle breeze.

"God's in heaven and all's right with the world," remarked Bill.

"It's days like this when we really need to stop and count our blessings," added Ralph.

"You're both right," said Sue, the board chairperson. "And one of our blessings is our church right down there," she exclaimed, pointing to the 128-year-old red brick structure with the tall white steeple. "Just look at the cemetery. Think of all of our families and friends who settled here and even built that first sanctuary. What a legacy they left us! That cemetery must be filled with stories of hard work and love and faith."

"Yep," said Bill.

"Uh, huh," agreed Ralph, eager to finish their hike.

However, Sue, wanting to continue the discussion, asked, "Wonder what would happen if this bridge suddenly collapsed under our combined weight. I wonder what it would be like if we fell and, well, that was it. We would be laid out in coffins side by side, in our church narthex, waiting for our funerals to begin. What would you like folks to say about you when they passed by on the way to their pews?"

"I haven't really given it much thought," Bill said as he looked longingly at their car parked at the other side of the bridge. "I guess I'd want folks to say I was a good husband and father, I worked hard, and I loved Jesus. What about you, Sue?"

"Well," began Sue. "I'd like folks to say I was a good worker for the Lord, I loved my family, and heaven is a wonderful place. What about you, Ralph? You've been pretty quiet. What would you like people to say about you when you're all stretched out in your coffin?"

"Well," sighed Ralph, "I'd like folks to say, 'Look! He's moving!' "

What would you like folks to say about you? About your community? About your congregation? How do you speak about yourselves? Your community? Are most of your verbs in the past tense? Do you spend most of your time thinking about what it was like in the past? Do you often grumble about the present and yearn for a future that will never be? Do your memories of a glorious and cherished past seem to be gone forever? Do you sometimes feel so used up and dried up that you have given up all hope?

Some scholars claim that congregations belonging to mainline denominations are now on the decline, watching life from the sidelines, reacting with a ho-hum line, and rapidly descending to flat line. "They have become dried up, helpless, and hopeless… just like the bones in Ezekiel's vision" (Ezekiel 37:1-2).

Do folks pass by your church building perceiving it as a coffin, holding the remains of a once vital ministry?

Does the exclamation, "Look, he's moving," apply to you or your congregation? How would you respond if the Lord asked you the same question the Lord put to Ezekiel: "Mortal, can these bones live?" (Ezekiel 37:3). The Lord promised the dry bones, "I will put my spirit within you and you shall live" (Ezekiel 37:14). What would that look like here? For you? For your parish?

The crucial word in today's lesson is "spirit" or in Hebrew, "ruah." It can also be translated as "breath" or "wind" (Ezekiel 37:5, 9-10). When God breathes life into even the driest and most brittle bones, they are filled with God's life-giving spirit. With a breath of fresh air, God's spirit, they begin to move with new life, new hope, and new energy.

Let's look more closely at today's lesson in Ezekiel. Its setting is in the midst of a fifty-year exile in Babylonia. After a long siege and fierce fighting, Jerusalem was overcome by Babylonian troops under King Nebuchadnezzar. Its city walls were nothing but rubble. The magnificent temple was in ruins. Its leading citizens were taken captive 500 miles away. The scene Ezekiel describes is the desolate plain where the refugees were settled... a place where battles had been fought; a place of death and devastation. Here in this place hopes were dashed, life was helpless despair, energy was dried up. It seemed as if even God had abandoned God's own people.

As Ezekiel gazed upon this tragic scene, the Lord asked him, "Mortal, can these bones live?" Well, Ezekiel was smart enough to avoid giving a wrong answer, so he replied, "O Lord God, you know" (Ezekiel 37:3). Perhaps the Lord is asking this same question to you. "Mortals, can this grieving family begin to revive? Mortals, can these dried up and apathetic Christians find renewed energy? Mortals, can the burdened bones not just survive, but even thrive?"

And your answer is... with Ezekiel, "O Lord God, you know." God did know and God did act, showing Ezekiel just what God's breath of fresh air could do. God is breathing fresh air into our lives even now. God is reviving that which was dry and dead: dead hope, dead faith, dead community, dead lives. God breathes ruah-spirit and suddenly "Look, they're moving"... moving with new life, new hope, and new energy.

That is God's promise to you, to the church, and to all dry bones: "I will put my spirit in you and you shall live." A breath of fresh air from the Lord does indeed give new life to a spiritually, emotionally, physically, and relationally drained and dry people. Hey, does that describe anybody you see when you look in the mirror? When you look at your congregation?

The Lord told Ezekiel that the dry bones really were the community of Israel. After the defeat at Jerusalem and their deportation to Babylonia, they had given up all hope of re-uniting with friends and family back home. They had given up hope of ever again being a chosen nation of the Lord. "They say our bones are dried up and our hope is lost. We are cut off completely" (Ezekiel 37:11). It was easy for them to hear only empty promises based on false possibilities. It also is easy for us to give up any hope for even the tiniest whisper of fresh air.

However, in scripture, hope is more than a remote possibility that something nearly impossible might happen — as in "I hope that I will win the lottery." In scripture, especially in today's text, hope is the sure and certain anticipation and expectation of what God has done, is doing, and promises to continue to do with and for God's people. Hope is given through the breath of fresh air... and the Spirit that God has given to us. Hope includes the wisdom to see things as they are and the vision to see what they will become when the Lord breathes on them.

What does hope look like when dry bones are connected, muscles develop, skin grows, and God's breath fills them? (Ezekiel 37:7-10). Look at the font and the splash of Jesus' love that connects and renews. Look at the altar and the nourishment of Jesus himself that feeds the soul. Look at the cross and the love of Jesus that spills out and fills empty hearts. Look at the gathered people around you and gaze at the memorial gifts throughout your building. You are surrounded by a great cloud of witnesses who now live in the reality of hope coming to pass in your midst. A breath of fresh air from the Lord reduces exhaustion and renews energy for even the driest bones. There's a story about a group of senior/seasoned citizens who were on a bus tour in Switzerland. They stopped at a farm, famous for its cheese made from goat's milk. Pointing to a small herd of goats in a nearby field the guide said, "Those are older goats, put out to pasture when they are too old to produce milk. What do you in America do with your old goats?"

With a twinkle in her eye one woman remarked, "They send us on bus tours of Switzerland and let us live in Sun City."

What happens when congregations seem to be drained of all vitality and vibrancy?

What do you do when you run out of energy? What happens to dry bones when the Lord breathes new life into them? God's breath of fresh air is more than a bus tour and a rocking chair for God's people.

What signs of new life and energy do you see around you at home, in your parish?

God's exiled people were so dried up that they couldn't see anything but devastation and couldn't feel anything but isolation. They needed Ezekiel to open their eyes and to help them feel the wind of the spirit as the Lord was breathing new life into their souls.

Friends, Ezekiel reminds you that the wind of God's Spirit is blowing in your midst today... giving you new life, new hope, new energy. Open your eyes to see what that looks like. Open your arms to show others what that feels like.

Hear again God's promise to the exiles in Babylonia and to you: "I will put my spirit within you and you shall live."

In Christ, let all God's people say, "Look, we're moving!" Amen.

Peace and Quiet
in an Upside-Down World

Johnny is four years old and he stopped taking naps before his second birthday. From his 6:15 am wake up (all by himself, no alarm clocks) until his 8 pm bed time, Johnny is in perpetual motion. He is running or talking or both all day long, and he expects the same from everyone around him. You can't be around Johnny very long without feeling exasperated and exhausted, yearning for just a few minutes of peace and quiet. You may know Johnny, or someone just like him.

One Sunday after church Johnny's Dad was attempting to read the newspaper and Johnny, well, Johnny was being Johnny. Finally, Dad had reached his tolerance limit. Seeing a full size map of the world on one page of the paper, Dad had an idea.

"Johnny," he said, "You have a map of the world on your bedroom wall, don't you?"

"Yeah Dad, right between my pictures of Jesus and my picture of the Ohio State Buckeye football team!" Johnny exclaimed.

Showing him the map on his newspaper page, Dad said to Johnny, "Here is something really fun. See this map of the world? I'm going to tear it in pieces, just like a puzzle." As Dad began to tear the world in small pieces, Johnny eagerly declared, "I'm really good at tearing paper." and jumped in to help. Pretty soon Johnny and his Dad had the world in many pieces on the living room floor.

"Now here's my chance for some peace and quiet," thought Dad. "Johnny, let's pretend that these pieces of paper are puzzle pieces of the world. Your job is to put the world back together."

"Okay," said Johnny as he started to do just that on the living room floor.

"Not here Johnny," Dad replied. "Take the puzzle into your bedroom and let the picture on the wall help you figure out where the pieces belong."

As Johnny was scooping up the torn scraps of paper, Dad was imagining at least ten quiet minutes; maybe even longer if Johnny didn't ask his mom to help out.

Well, you can guess what happened. Before Dad could even finish reading last night's basketball scores, Johnny burst into the living room, jumped on Dad's lap, and cried out, "I'm all finished! Come and see! Come and see!"

With a sigh, Dad slowly pushed himself up out of his recliner and asked Johnny, "How did you do this so quickly? I thought that I would have more time to… oops, I mean that you would need more time to finish the puzzle."

With a gleam in his eye, Johnny said, "I gave up. I couldn't do the world by myself, Dad, so I turned those pieces upside down. On the other side was a picture of Jesus on the cross. When I put Jesus back where he belonged, the pieces of the world came together too! Quick, come and see!"

Hand in hand, Dad and Johnny stared quietly, in holy silence at Jesus Christ crucified. Peace and quiet in an upside-down world! Here is a wonderful description of Holy Week that begins today, Palm Sunday. The crucified Christ holds the world together. Christ on the cross turns the values of the world upside down. The suffering of Christ shatters the way the world defines meaning.

Today, Palm Sunday, is a day in the church calendar when God clearly shows us what it looks like to follow Jesus. This day begins a week when our focus shifts from what we want, what we need, and what we must do, to what God has done, is doing, and continues to do. During this week God moves us beyond our expectations and into God's own promises.

Today begins with palms of praise for Jesus and concludes with the reality of the passionate suffering of Jesus. Today many children wave palm branches as Christians enter places of worship. During the service they might twist these same branches into a cross. It is the horrible and shameful cross, not the branches of the royal palm that God has made into the mark of victory over evil. During this week, the holiest of weeks, the week when God turned the world upside down, God twists leaves of palm into a cross of triumph. Our palm branches today will become the ashes of mourning placed on our foreheads next year on Ash Wednesday.

Our lesson from Isaiah adds some depth to help us grasp the holy and awesome power of this week. In this text, God reverses the world's expectations of success and shows what true faithfulness really looks like. Here Isaiah is addressing Jews who are living as exiles in Babylonia hundreds of miles from home. Their nation had been conquered, their city devastated, and their temple destroyed. They had become an object of ridicule to other nations. Shame permeated their thoughts. Their world was in pieces. Their only reality was daily suffering and humiliation. Here, Isaiah's words turn that world upside down. Here, Isaiah presents specific examples of what God's gift of faithfulness would look like to the exiles, to you, to your congregation, and to all God's people.

First, is the tongue of a teacher (Isaiah 50:4). Now, all prophets, including Isaiah, had many students; disciples who studied with them and expected to pass on to others the wisdom learned at their master's feet. As Jesus learned from the Father, so did he teach his disciples, who in turn taught others. Faithfulness is passing on to others the wisdom learned at the master's feet.

Second, faithful teaching first means faithful listening to the master every day. "Morning by morning he wakens — wakens my ear to listen as those who were taught" (Isaiah 50:4). For Isaiah's disciples there and then and for Jesus' disciples here and now, faithfulness includes daily listening to the master. Have you ever heard a good teacher remark that they never really understood a skill or concept very well until they were required to teach it? Did you know that many medical schools train physicians using a "see it — do it — teach it" methodology? Many seminaries utilize that same model.

Try something this week. Morning by morning, read the scripture lessons your congregation will use during Holy Week. Then take a moment to reflect on what the Lord is showing you about yourself, your congregation, your community. If possible, try this exercise with another person. You could do this together, or even "on-line" via email or other social networking sights. Faithfulness includes both the ear and tongue of the teacher.

Third, what specifically do you hear and teach? Why does God give us "the tongue of a teacher"? Isaiah states, "… that I might know how to sustain the weary with a word" (Isaiah 50:4). Who are the weary and exhausted around you? Who are the exasperated and frustrated? Who are the grieving and lonely? Who are the oppressed and despised? Who are the sick and suffering? Who are the humiliated and ashamed? Perhaps you consider yourself described here as well.

So, then how can you sustain these folks when you are also losing your own strength to carry on? What possible word can sustain you yourself, let alone others?

In the language of the Old Testament, *dabar*, or "word," also means "force" or "thing." The spoken word contains a tangible power within it. We have all heard the childhood retort to personal insult: "Sticks and stones will break my bones but words will never hurt me." Most of us still, literally, feel the pain from taunts we heard years, even decades ago. However, the sustaining word is a loving action. For example, John's gospel begins like this: "In the beginning was the word and the word was with God and the word was God" (John 1:1). Then John writes, "and the word became flesh and dwelt among us" (John 1:14). This "word" was actually God's own person, living among us. The word itself became the loving presence of God in our midst.

When seminary students begin their ten week hospital training most are afraid that they will not know what words to say during crisis situations. Quickly they learn that sustaining the weary with a word often looks like providing a comforting and compassionate presence when no words are possible. "Don't say something, just stand there!" they are advised by supervising chaplains. "Don't babble words, re-present God's Word (Jesus)," they hear from professors. Who needs to be sustained with God's word in your congregation?

Finally, we cannot be faithful on our own. As Isaiah proclaims in the midst of vicious insults and brutal ridicule, "The Lord God helps me. Therefore, I have not been disgraced" (Isaiah 50:5-7). The Lord does indeed give us the courage and determination to face impossible obstacles so that we can declare with Isaiah, "I have set my face like flint and I know that I shall not be put to shame" (Isaiah 50:7).

Can you see the Passion / Palm Sunday Jesus in this text from Isaiah? Can you see Jesus here in the willing suffering? In his face set like flint marching firmly and into Jerusalem (Luke 9:51)? In listening to his father as he kneels in the garden and breathes his last on the cross?

We can't be faithful on our own. Only Jesus did that. However, like the one in our lesson, we are not left alone to cope with suffering. Four times in these five verses Isaiah reminds us; the Lord God gives the tongue of a teacher (v. 1), the Lord God opens our ears (v. 1); the Lord God helps me (vv. 7, 9).

Today we see the Lord God helping us, sustaining us, teaching us, and inviting us to share his life-changing journey to the cross. Today begins the week when the Lord God turns our broken and fragmented world upside down and rearranges its pieces into a cross of love and a face of forgiveness. Today God begins a week of show-and-tell that changed the world forever. Amen.

Maundy Thursday
Exodus 12:1-4 (5-10) 11-14

Remembering Then;
Anticipating When

Today is called Maundy Thursday by Christians through-out the world. As some of you may already know, "Maundy" is an English form of *mandatum*, the Latin word for com-mandment. The scripture theme for this day comes from Jesus celebrating a Passover meal with his disciples on the night that Jesus was betrayed. Here Jesus told them, "I give you a new commandment; that you love one another. Just as I have loved you, you also should love one another" (John 13:34, see also John 15:12-17).

Maundy Thursday is a time for remembering what God's love looked like in Bible times, what that new love looks like now in our lives, and anticipating what God's ultimate love will look like when we celebrate resurrection.

In today's scripture lesson, God's love was remembered on a particular day by a family meal with specific foods pre-pared with precise instructions. It was to be consumed in haste with detailed actions and in the most reverent man-ner, even with instructions on how to get rid of the leftovers. Roast the meat. Don't boil it (v. 9). Don't use any kind of leavening agent (like yeast) when you bake the bread (v. 8). Burn up all your leftovers first thing in the morning (v. 10). Eat quickly, and be dressed and ready to move out as fast as possible, so keep your shoes on and your walking stick close by (v. 11).

Why was all this elaborate attention given to what seemed to be the most trivial? God wanted God's people to remem-ber the pivotal event that demonstrated God's love for them.

To remember then meant sharing the story of deliverance from slavery in Egypt. To remember then meant recalling how God told their ancestors to sprinkle some blood on the doorway posts from the lamb sacrificed for the meal. Then the angel of the Lord would pass over and spare these households, striking only the Egyptians with a destroying plague (vv. 7, 13). Remembering the blood meant recognizing that the blood of the lamb was not simply a sign of God's love for a particular household; the blood was a sign of God's forever love promised to all of Israel. Blood was recognized as life both given and received by God; as vitality created and continued in God.

Remembering Passover was so crucial for the Hebrews that they even used today's text to begin a new calendar. All of Israel's history was to be dated from their deliverance from slavery (v. 2).

Jesus and his disciples also gathered to eat and remember God's mighty saving act. As they remembered then, they began to recognize what they were facing now, and perhaps even to anticipate what it would be like when this week would end. Perhaps they read aloud the verses of today's text as the meal was prepared and shared. Perhaps they tarried a bit over the words, "The blood shall be a sign for you on the house where you live, when I see the blood I will pass over you" (v. 13). Perhaps a few weeks later the disciples remembered the blood of Jesus on the cross and recognized the blood of God's new Passover lamb.

Remembering God's love helps us to recognize God's new love now and to anticipate God's promise of love when all is fulfilled.

Today in many congregations, Christians show what the servant love of Christ looks like through the washing of one another's feet (John 13:12-17). Most Christians will remember Jesus' last supper with his disciples as they celebrate Holy Communion. Here the unleavened bread and the roasted lamb become the body of Christ, the Lamb of God. Here the lamb's blood sprinkled on door posts become the saving blood of Christ. Here, the Lamb of God speaks to us, "This is my body that is for you. Do this in remembrance of me... this cup is the new covenant in my blood Do this as often as you drink it in rememberance of me" (1 Corinthians 11:24-25).

In our text for Maundy Thursday God reminds us that "This day shall be a day of remembrance for you. You shall celebrate it as a festival to the Lord" (Exodus 12:14). We are gathering. We are celebrating. We are remembering what God has done to deliver us from bondage, recognizing what God is doing now to love and nurture us on our life journey, and anticipating when God will invite us to partake in the final feast of victory with all the saints.

So, what does all this mean for us today? What does Jesus' new commandment look like right now in our congregation and community? What does it mean for us to remember then and to anticipate when?

First, each time we gather to share the communion meal, we are not simply remembering Jesus' life and death. We are receiving new life from him. We are being nurtured and sustained by him. We are participating with all of God's people in God's saving deliverance from all bondage to slavery and sin.

Second, each time we gather we are proclaiming the love of Christ to others. Paul writes, "For as often as you eat this bread and drink this cup, you proclaim the Lord's death until he comes" (1 Corinthians 11:26). Here we join "a great cloud of witnesses" (Hebrews 12:1) who surround us and inspire us to show God's love as a gift given to us, a body broken for us, blood spilled to deliver us.

Third, each time God gathers us to remember, God also sends us out to show what this new commandment of love looks like beyond church doors. Here's an old fable often shared in graduate courses in counseling and group psychotherapy. It is also a good demonstration of the new commandment of love Jesus gave to his disciples. It goes like this:

A holy man was contemplating what heaven and hell might look like. Suddenly he had a vision in which the Lord led him to two doors. The holy man opened the first door and saw a larger round table in the center of the room. A large pot of deliciously smelling stew sat in the middle of the table. The people sitting around the table were very thin and sickly. Their groaning filled the room. They looked like they were starving, even though that mouth watering stew was in their midst.

As the holy man watched, he noticed that these people were holding spoons with very long handles that seemed to be chained to their arms. Each one could reach into the pot and get a spoonful of stew. However, because the handle was longer than their arms, they were unable to get the spoons into their mouths. The holy man was deeply sadden at their misery.

"Now you have had a vision of hell," said the Lord. "Now open the second door."

When he entered, the holy man noticed that the room was exactly the same as the first. In the middle of the room was a large round table with the large delicious stew pot in the center. The people sitting around the table were fitted with the same long handled spoons. However, in this room the people were well nourished. Their laughter filled the room.

"Now you have seen heaven," the Lord said.

"But I don't understand, Lord," the holy man replied.

"Well," explained the Lord, "it's really pretty simple. In hell, people only think of themselves and try to satisfy their own wants and needs. They don't love each other. They don't even like each other. They certainly don't see that they need each other. As a result, nobody is satisfied. Everybody is miserable all the time... forever. Now watch closely. Notice that the people in this room are feeding each other. They may not always like each other, but they know that they need each other, and have begun to see that this is what it's like to love each other."

And Jesus said, "I give you a new commandment, that you love one another... by this everyone will know that you are my disciples, if you have love for one another."

— John 13:34-35

What does this new commandment look like for you? For your congregation? What might everyone see when they enter the doors of your home? What will they remember? What might everyone see when they walk through the doors of your church for the first time? What will they remember? What happens with the overflowing love of Christ that is in your midst? What will they remember? What will you share?

This is Maundy Thursday. As the Lord tells us in our text, "This shall be a day of remembrance for you" (v. 14). This is a day to remember the Lord's deliverance from slavery and bondage. This is a day to taste and to share the Lord's loving acts. This is a day to anticipate the incredible joy when Christ shares the full banquet feast with us forever. Amen.

Good Friday
Isaiah 52:13—53:12

What Does Jesus Look Like?

Jenny had spent the past half hour working quietly all by herself at the art table in her Sunday school classroom. This was unusual behavior for any three-year-old child, but for this gregarious extrovert it was extraordinary. When class time was over, Jenny's parents came in to take her to the sanctuary for worship.

"Come on Jenny, it's time for church," said Mom. Jenny just shook her head and continued with her crayon drawing.

"Jenny, we have to get moving," added her father.

"Just a minute, I'm almost done," Jenny pleaded.

With a familiar sigh and a quick glance at her watch, Mom told Jenny, "Okay, just one minute. But hurry up. What are you drawing that's so important anyway?"

"I'm drawing a picture of Jesus," exclaimed Jenny proudly.

Shaking his head Jenny's dad said, "Jenny, nobody knows exactly what Jesus looks like."

"They will in a minute!" proclaimed Jenny, and got back to work.

Can you guess what this precocious young lady was drawing? You are absolutely correct… Jenny was not drawing a face. She was making a cross using every one of the 64 crayons in the art table box!

Indeed, especially on Good Friday, the cross gives us a most holy lens for observing what Jesus looks like and loves like. Our Old Testament lesson offers some focus.

Who is this servant Isaiah mentions anyway? Is he Isaiah or one of his disciples? Could it be Cyrus of Persia? How about the population of Hebrews living as exiles in Babylonia? Or the whole nation of Israel? Or even Jesus himself? So, what does Jesus look like? What does this servant look like?

Trying to figure this out is like trying to nail a drop of water to a window pane. It can't be done, and it doesn't really matter. Isaiah states that the appearance of God's servant would not stand out in a crowd. In fact, this servant is after one "from whom others would hide their faces" (Isaiah 53:3).

So, today, on this Good Friday, we might be able to get a glimpse of what Jesus looks like by looking at Isaiah's description of what the servant did and what were the results. As you hear Isaiah's words here, keep in your minds Jenny's cross of 64 colors. Keep in your hearts God's servant who was nailed there.

Here is Jesus. Here is how Isaiah describes him. He was despised and rejected (v. 3), oppressed and afflicted (v. 7), wounded (v. 5) and crushed (v. 10), cut off and stricken (v. 8) for us. Here is the one whom we name Jesus, the one whom Isaiah names God's servant, who has borne our infirmities and carried our diseases (Isaiah 53:4). Here is the one whose "punishment made us whole, and by his bruises we are healed" (Isaiah 53:4). Now can you see how Isaiah's description begins to help Jenny's picture come alive?

Why did all this happen? Why do we look at Jesus through this lens of suffering? Well, God's people couldn't seem to stop their endless cycle of sin and disobedience. No priestly sacrifice could break this pattern. Left on their own God's people were helpless and their efforts were hopeless.

So God took the initiative to break this pattern. God began to bring into focus an even sharper picture of the depth of God's own passion for the world. In Jesus Christ, God's love entered the world and lived in the midst of the people (John 1:14). In Jesus Christ, God's innocent, kind, and compassionate servant, God chose to defeat the control of sin and suffering.

Aha! Now even more detail can be added to Jenny's multi-colored drawing. In addition to a body tormented with suffering, we can also see a heart filled with love, eyes over flowing with compassion, and arms outstretched with an embrace for the whole world. Today, Good Friday, God shows us what love looked like on the cross. Today, Jenny's multi-colored drawing invites us to see what God's love can look like from the cross into the midst of our daily lives.

As you know well, suffering is still very real. Each one of us has personal experience with affliction and rejection. Nevertheless, the Good Friday sin and suffering are no longer in control. They no longer have power over us. Christ has defeated them forever, turning an emblem of suffering into a brilliant cross of triumph. There are living witnesses among us whom God is using to show us what that victory looks like every day.

Mitzi was suffering from a severe and crippling arthritis in her spine. It had become so bad that she was in constant pain, able to get around only in a wheelchair. One day her pastor asked her how she could keep going and stay so courageous in the midst of constant pain.

"Well, Pastor," Mitzi began, "Every time I hurt I think of Jesus on the cross. You know, it seems like he and I are a lot closer since the pain started."

Right on, Mitzi!

Marilyn was a young Army officer on the fast track toward captain's bars when she was diagnosed with a painful, debilitating, and chronic disease that strikes connective tissue between joints. It would eventually impact her entire body including the brain. As her agony increased during the next few months, Marilyn grew increasingly depressed. One evening, all alone, she took a bottle full of sleeping pills and went to bed fully expecting to die. Shortly after midnight a neighbor backed her car into Marilyn's automobile in the parking lot, causing both vehicles to burst into flame. When Marilyn didn't respond to the apartment manager's phone call, he rushed to her unit and discovered Marilyn unconscious and near death.

The resulting hospitalization led Marilyn to begin a new vocation as a therapist working with persons unable to cope with traumatic and painful experiences. When folks ask Marilyn what changed for her, she stated, "I discovered that I can't change the fact that I have pain. I can't control the reality that I do suffer. However, what I can control is how I suffer" and pointing to the cross on her desk, Marilyn adds, "that cross shows me every day that God understands my pain because God's Son suffered too."

That cross shows how deeply and faithfully God loves Mitzi, Marilyn, and all God's children. On that cross, Jesus did what no human can do… stop the control that suffering and sin have on our lives. Of course sin and suffering still exist. Of course grief and pain are still part of life. Of course violence and injustice create new victims by the hour. However, thanks to Jesus, the crucified servant Son of God, their pattern of control in our lives has ended.

Thanks to Jenny's drawing we can see a beautiful, communal tapestry of all God's children united together through a 64 crayon cross. Thanks to this really Good Friday vision of Jesus we can see hope and possibility where others see only ugliness and worthlessness. On this Good Friday we begin to see the sacred and holy in the midst of the mundane and ordinary. On God's Good Friday, we begin to see God seeking after the lost when others see only the lost. Today, on God's Good and Awesome Friday, we see God's presence in the lonely and despised, the broken and forgotten, when others shut their eyes in hopeless despair.

Today we have a glimpse of what Jesus looks like. Although despised and wounded he was also exalted and lifted up. Although he was afflicted and oppressed, he was still kind and compassionate. Today we see what Jesus looks like, suffering the cost of our sin with a love so deep and so passionate that we are startled into silent, awesome wonder as we gaze at the cross. Today really is Good Friday.

Thanks Jenny.

Thanks Isaiah.

Thanks Jesus. Amen.

What Difference Does it Make?

What a joyful day! Throughout the world Christians are gathered to celebrate resurrection… new life emerging from the grave; new light bursting forth from a darkened tomb.

Throughout the world Christians celebrate as the cross of a suffering, bleeding, dying Jesus is now surrounded by dancing children waiting their turn to decorate it with brightly colored spring flowers. Throughout the world, churches are filled with Christians shouting back and forth "Christ is risen! He is risen indeed! Alleluia!" Christians are rejoicing and splashing in welcoming baptismal waters. They are tasting the nurturing and forgiving presence of Jesus himself in bread broken and wine poured. Christians gather with anticipation of new life and sing with excitement at the promise of new hope.

So, what about those folks on the outside looking in at all these happy people? What difference does all this make to them? What about those folks driving by the church on their way to the golf course, soccer games, family picnics, or home improvement stores? What difference does it make to those who are living in cardboard boxes? To those who are waking up with drug or alcohol hangovers? To those who live in constant fear of being beaten by a family member? To those in harm's way in distant lands? To those whose families are broken by bitterness and misunderstanding? To those who are excluded and ridiculed because of their race or gender or nationality?

You know, in many churches today, there are folks who just don't get this Christian stuff. They are physically here, all right, but still feel like they are on the outside looking in — kind of like being a spectator at a game you don't really understand or even care about very much. Even the most devoted church members would acknowledge these feelings at times.

What difference does all this Easter stuff really make in my life anyway? What difference does it make in the world? Just look around and watch television. Read the newspapers. Check out world events on the internet. The world's in a mess. What Easter difference can Christians possibly make? We show up, put on happy faces in the parking lot, say the right words of greeting in the narthex, go through the proper worship motions in the sanctuary, and then return home to the same old way of thinking and behaving.

Can you guess what word most non-church members use to describe Christians? You are exactly right if you guessed "hypocrite." We are indeed guilty of saying one thing and doing just the opposite. We are often guilty of speaking with sincerity and preaching with passion; yet acting as if we are more "religious" than anyone else. We behave without understanding the experience of others. It's as if we are trapped in a tomb of our own making.

Carl was a newly ordained pastor preparing for his first journey through the season of Lent with his new parishioners. As most new pastors, Carl struggled with time management. There just weren't enough hours in the day to prepare for all those extra sermons and classes and meals. Worship services needed extra attention too. Carl wanted everything to be just right for everybody. He needed folks to see that this would be the most meaningful Lenten season ever. Carl's plans were meticulous. He was ready to be holy for his people.

However, the week before Ash Wednesday was filled with unexpected parish crises and wouldn't you just know it, Carl had a sinus infection. An hour before Ash Wednesday worship would begin Carl discovered that he had forgotten to prepare the ashes for marking the cross on parishioner's foreheads. The youth group had burned palm branches all right but they were too dry. He recalled that he learned in seminary that a small amount of olive oil should be mixed with ashes first. Frantically racing to the church kitchen, Carl searched everywhere for olive oil or any kind of oil... but to no avail. Seeing the water fountain, Carl thought, "Oh, what difference does it make anyway... as long as the ashes are wet."

Well, the story of that Ash Wednesday many years ago is still told in Carl's first parish. You see, the difference between a mixture of olive oil and ashes and a mixture of water and ashes of palm is a painful and caustic difference. The first mixture is a harmless paste. The second is a burning adhesive.

Fortunately, only a very few people (including Pastor Carl) experienced the pain before the mistake was obvious and the rite was halted.

What difference did this make to Carl? Busted! Humiliated! Guilty as charged! Hypocrite!... intending a careful and intentional sign of God's love but resulting in a careless and accidental demonstration of pastoral inadequacy. Can hypocrites make any difference in the world?

Let's look at the example of one of history's best known hypocrite; Peter, disciple of Jesus. Jesus complimented Peter for his confession that Jesus was the Messiah, the Son of God (Matthew 16:15-19). Then, when Jesus clearly explained that his plan of salvation involved going to Jerusalem, suffering, dying, and being raised.... well Peter had the audacity to rebuke Jesus for this foolish mission (Matthew 16:22). Jesus told Peter to get out of the way, calling Peter selfish, a stumbling block, and even Satan himself (Matthew 16:21-23). On the night of Jesus' arrest, Peter promised Jesus that he would never desert him (Matthew 26:33) and then immediately fell asleep during Jesus' agonizing prayer in the Garden of Gethsemane (Matthew 26:40-41). Hypocrite! Peter declared to Jesus, "Even though I must die with you, I will never deny you" (Matthew 26:35). A few hours later, Peter cursed in the shadows and denied Jesus three times (Matthew 26:64-72).

Hypocrite! Sinner! Jesus did not give up on Peter. He does not give up on us. Sometime after that first Easter morning Peter became a leader among the first Christians teaching, healing, and preaching the good news of a risen, living, and forgiving Savior. However, in Peter's mind, there was a hitch — a condition to meet. There was a test to pass before you could receive God's love and forgiveness.

To be acceptable to God and become part of this new Easter community you needed to obey Jewish dietary and other religious laws including circumcision. If you would not do this, you were not clean enough to receive God's gift. You were unclean and profane (Acts 10:14). And that's the way it was. That described Christians 2,000 years ago. Sadly, that describes some Christians today. It will describe Christians in the future... trapped in a tomb of sin and hypocrisy that we cannot escape without God's help.

So here is the Easter difference. Today, God takes over. Today, God rolls back the stone from the tomb that keeps us helplessly trapped within our own sin. Today, God sets us free from prisons we have built for ourselves. Christ is risen. He is risen indeed! Alleluia!

God shows us how others may see us. He also shows us how we may really see ourselves — sinners trapped in our own hypocrisy. God shows us how God see us: forgiven, loved, and free to show others what that looks like.

The story of Peter and Cornelius in Acts 10 gives us a specific, difference-making, hypocrisy-shattering example of what resurrected living in Christ looks like.

The chapter begins with Cornelius, a Roman army officer who was already on the fringe of the faithful community.

As Luke writes, "Cornelius was a devout man who feared God with all his household; he gave alms generously to the people and prayed continually to God" (Acts 10:2). Yet Cornelius and his household were like many sincere, moral, caring people today; they were on the outside looking in at the faithful. As Gentiles, they were unclean; however, because they prayed and gave alms and believed in God, they were sort of "almost-but-not-quite" clean. They could not become Jews without first observing strictly proscribed dietary laws and following specific religious rites that included circumcision. They couldn't become Christians without first becoming Jews.

In many Christian congregations there are people who find themselves on the outside looking in; welcome to stay and pray and obey and pay... but not really welcome to become part of the living and resurrected community of the church.

God rolled the stone away from that tomb all right! An angel came to Cornelius and told him to send for Peter (Acts 10:3-4). Yes, that Peter; the hypocrite Peter, the one who would not touch any unclean food or even enter the house of any unclean person.

At the same time God showed Peter a tomb-shattering, difference-making vision of Easter reality. "What God has made clean, you must not call profane" (Acts 10:15). Here is the Easter difference. God rolls away the hypocritical and exclusive blinders many Christians wear these days, just like Peter wore in those days. God gave Peter a new and faithful way to understand Gentiles. God gave Cornelius and his household a new and faithful way to understand Christians. Today, God is doing that for us.

Then God brought them together, just as God brings us together today. In fact, simply by entering Cornelius' house and meeting with his friends and relatives Peter had already broken a religious law that had previously blocked his understanding and restricted his mission and his message in Christ's name (Acts 10:28).

So, what was that difference making message? Peter already showed it by his behavior. Now, finally, in our text, Peter tells it this way: "I truly understand that God shows no partiality... anyone who fears him and does what is right is acceptable to him" (Acts 10:28-29).

In Jesus God opens us to see that oppression, suffering, and hypocrisy are no longer in control. Christ rolled the tombstone away from that mess. Christ sends us, with Peter, into the very spaces and places we would rather forget. Christ sends us into the very households of people who look, think, and act differently.

You know, it still is pretty difficult for us church folk to really grasp this. We do get stuck in the same rut pretty often, don't we? Retired Clemson University football coach Frank Howard was once asked if he thought that rowing would ever become a collegiate varsity sport. "No way," exclaimed the legendary coach. "Any activity that requires people to sit on their backsides and move backward isn't worthy to be called a sport in my book."

Well, some folks who see themselves on the outside looking in at church members may say the same thing about Christians.

Remember Pastor Carl? Well, on Easter Sunday he retold the story of the Ash Wednesday debacle. Of course, it had already spread throughout the small community where his congregation was located. In his sermon Pastor Carl admitted his error and confessed that his own need to impress people got in the way of faithful actions. Carl stated that he had often been so strapped by his own personal desire to be liked and approved that he could not free himself. It was like living in his own personal tomb. That Easter, Christ rolled away the stone that had trapped Carl in a life of phoniness and artificial religiosity. Christ rolled away the stone that separated pastor and people.

Today, Christ rolls away the stone from tombs that keep us from seeing all people as clean and acceptable creatures of God who shows no partiality. Today, with Peter, and all the other hypocrites and forgiven sinners, Christ opens us to a love that makes a difference. Today Christ dances in our midst, sings in our souls, and sends us to serve. Christ is risen! He is risen indeed! Alleluia! Amen.

Named, Claimed, and Framed

So, here we are just over one week after Easter Sunday. Vigils are finished. Sunrise services are over. Dishes from the youth breakfast have been washed and put away. Brass and tympani fanfares have concluded. Flowers on the cross have begun to wilt and blow away. Fewer pews are filled.

In most communities, spring break is over. Easter vacations have ended. The return of familiar routines begin. The joy of Easter is still there, but it has diminished somewhat with a return to "the real world." Nevertheless the antiphonal Easter proclamation continues. "Christ is risen. He is risen indeed. Alleluia!" Did you notice just a tad bit less enthusiasm?

Christ's resurrection is a reality. Yet it's impossible to maintain the emotional and spiritual highs of Easter morning. The excitement has disappeared. Now what?

It's tough being a follower of Jesus without uplifting music in the midst of a supportive community filled with optimistic hope. Life goes on. It was even more difficult to be a follower of Jesus in those first days after the resurrection. In our text for today and for the next two Sundays we will see how the Holy Spirit used Peter to help folks remain faithful as they returned to their daily routines and challenges.

Today, our text describes what it means to be an after-Easter people. Next Sunday's first lesson presents what God wants after-Easter people to do. Two weeks from today, Peter's address concludes with a description of how after-Easter people are to live.

Here's a familiar story.

A weary mother returned from the store with her arms filled with groceries. She was greeted at the door by her eight-year-old daughter Sally who couldn't wait to tell what her little brother, Timmy, had done. "Daddy was on the phone and I was out playing," she began. "Timmy took his new crayons and wrote on the new wallpaper you just put up in the living room. I told him you'd be real mad."

"Oh my," said her mother with a long sigh, "Where's Timmy now?"

"He's inside the closet over there," answered Sally, pointing directly at the hiding place of her little brother.

"Timmy, come out here this instant," said his mother sternly. For the next five minutes she proceeded to scold Timmy for his lack of concern for others. She ranted about how he always seemed to act before he thought. Then she stomped into the living room, expecting to see the damage and confirm her worst fears. Instead, her eyes filled with tears. When Timmy's mom looked at the wall, in crayon, Timmy had printed, "I love my mommy." He had carefully surrounded his message with a large, red heart.

Rather than re-papering the wall, Timmy's parents decided to re-frame the message. Today, many years later, that living room wall remains just the same. However, Timmy's message is now surrounded by a beautiful picture frame. Whenever family members or guests see it they remember what it looks like to be surrounded by a powerful, welcoming, and forgiving love.

So, what does this mean for us as the routines of our daily lives begin to absorb us once again? Here is Peter's message to those first after-Easter people in our text and to those after-Easter people gathered here. How can we make sense now out of all those things that happened then?

Named. Peter's address here sets a foundation for a new and exciting chapter for followers of Jesus. They were becoming a brand new community. Soon they would also have a brand new name, "Christian" (Acts 11:26). Wherever and whenever they gathered, these after-Easter people of God would be named "Church" (Colossians 1:24) or "Body of Christ" (1 Corinthians 12:27).

Claimed. God's action in Jesus claims us as God's own people. As Peter declares in our text, those first after-Easter people had seen the "powers, wonders, and signs that God had done through Jesus" (Acts 2:22) in their midst. These miracles of Jesus were signs that the kingdom of God was near and that God had claimed them as part of it. And then everything ended in disaster. The Messiah they expected would certainly not be tortured and killed by the same Roman enemy he was supposed to defeat. The Messiah they expected certainly would not be betrayed and put on trial by their fellow Israelites for, of all things, blatantly defaming God and disobeying the sacred laws of God's people.

It is tough being an after-Easter people. It was in those days. Is still is today. If God had indeed sent Jesus to usher in the messianic kingdom and claimed them as its charter members, this was a strange way of showing it. Sure, some folks, including Peter, said that Jesus' crucifixion "happened according to the definite plan and foreknowledge of God" (Acts 2:23). Somehow, this just doesn't seem to give enough courage or substance to get through the doubts and struggles of each day. More signs and wonders for the after-Easter people in the real world ASAP. Please!

Well, okay, there is Jesus' resurrection. Peter states, "God raised him up having freed him from death, because it was impossible for him to be held in its power" (Acts 2:24). However, that was many days ago. That really was a big celebration and emotional high; a real spiritual explosion. But now what? How do we really know God claims us for God's own people? Where's Jesus when you really need him?

Look around folks. Look at the baptismal font where God names you and claims you as God's beloved child forever. Here, with a splash, the Lord declares, "I have called you by name, you are mine" (Isaiah 43:1). Look at the altar, the table of the Lord. Here is precisely where Jesus is when you need him the most. Here is where Jesus gives himself to strengthen you in your daily after-Easter struggle. Here Jesus himself feeds you and tells you "This is my body, given for you. This is my blood, shed for you." Framed. We are forever named and claimed as God's own children, God's own after-Easter people. That's easy to say but even easier to forget in the real world. Anyone who enters Timmy's living room can see the framed reality of a love that continues to live in that family. God's after-Easter people also need a frame for remembering Jesus' love in the living spaces of their lives.

Matthew is almost three years old, and soon he will be the official big brother to Myra, who is still living comfortably in Mommy's tummy for a few more weeks. Matthew talks to Myra every night before bedtime. Matthew hugs Mommy's tummy and uses his deep, big brother voice to say, "Night, night Myra. I'm your big brother. I love you!"

Named, claimed, and framed. What a blessing for any baby sister about ready to begin a new chapter in life. Although not yet fully visible, Myra is already being named, claimed, framed, and loved into a new family.

On Loren and Ryan's computer monitor is a screen saver picture of their laughing eighteen-month-old son, Orin. His arms are wide open and ready to frame them with a loving embrace. Although not yet fully visible, God was embracing these first after-Easter people in today's text. As part of God's definite plan, God was truly loving them and framing them to a new family and a new community. Here God was framing a forever message of love that would connect God's past loving deeds with God's future promise of joyful presence… Quoting Psalm 16:8, Peter proclaims, "You have made known to me the ways of life; you will make me full of gladness with your presence" (Acts 2:28).

So, what does this frame look like and where is it anyway? Look around you. See God's claimed people gathered around God's own living word. Notice the table there. Gaze at the font over there. Now focus your attention on the cross. Imagine the outstretched arms of Jesus embracing it all; surrounding us all; framing and filling this new family with the joy of his presence.

After-Easter people remember that the crucified, dead, and buried Jesus is no longer trapped and framed by any time and space tomb. After-Easter people remember, as Peter declares, "This Jesus God raised up, and of that all of us are witnesses." God has included us, named and claimed after-Easter people, as witnesses to this new reality, members of this new community, part of the new frame that centers God's loving message for us and for the world forever.

God's framed future has begun — a new and living reality is becoming visible. The old is passing away. Death has lost its sting. Grief has lost its power. Sin has lost its control. Christ is risen! He is risen indeed! Alleluia! Amen.

Claimed, Framed, Changed

What do athletic coaches, politicians, and preachers have in common? They are expected to give inspirational pep talks, speeches, or sermons that fire up powerful emotions. They are supposed to motivate their listeners to "give 110%," overcoming all obstacles to victory no matter what the cost.

Coaches know that the best pep talk can only get athletes through the first football collision, the first gymnastics tumbling pass, or the first baseball at bat. Politicians know that the most stirring speech is forgotten when the auditorium clears or the channel is changed. Preachers know that emotions raised in the most energizing sermon quickly dissipate with the last chords of the final hymn.

Emotions fire and fizzle without a game plan. With specific directions to follow, athletes, voters, and parishioners find themselves trapped in an endless and random pattern of emotional highs and lows. It's the "same-old-same-old"; "almost-but-not-quite" search for meaning. It's the "woulda'-coulda'-shoulda — if-only" self-deceiving quest for success.

Today's text begins with the conclusion of what may have been the most inspiring and motivational address ever given by Peter. Peter had just described how God's plan of love was poured out for them by the crucifixion and resurrection of Jesus (Acts 2:14-35). Now Peter declares "with certainty that God has made him [Jesus] both Lord and messiah" (Acts 2:36). This fulfills God's game plan of salvation not just for everybody in the crowd but for all of Israel. God's promised Messiah had come to them and he was Jesus of Nazareth. God's promised Christ, Peter told them, was "this Jesus whom you crucified" (Acts 2:36).

Wow! That really fanned their emotional flames. Our text states that "when they heard this, they were cut to the heart" (Acts 2:37). In one powerful address, Peter had described how God still claimed them as God's own children, even though they killed their own God-given messiah. In one inspiring sermon Peter made clear how God still had placed them within the center of God's love, framed by the outstretched embrace of Christ crucified.

Of course the people were cut to the heart and stung to the soul. Of course they were deeply grieved and saddened when they experienced the full implication of Peter's words. Claimed by God, yes; framed within God's love, yes; but now they were brokenhearted (see Psalm 109:16) and stunned by their own past misguided behavior.

So, now what? What could they do about it all? What can you do when your emotions are stirred up? Well, you can ignore them and push them down deep inside and pretend they just don't exist. However, that doesn't work for very long. Emotions aren't imaginary. They remain in the brain. Somehow they will come out and show themselves. Like it or not. Push them down long enough and they will burst through our best efforts to keep them under control… just like a shaken up bottle of soda when the cap is removed. Sometimes this emotional spray looks like uncontrollable rage. Other times it looks like a flood of tears. Still other times, overwhelming emotions seek release through repeated physical symptoms.

Emotions are real. Being "cut to the heart" is powerful. However, the crowds who were listening to Peter did not ignore their emotions. They did not express them in violent outrage. Instead, the crowds acknowledged them and asked for help. In other words, they asked for a game plan saying to "Peter and the other apostles, 'Brothers, what should we do?'" (Acts 2:37).

This is also a crucial question for us today. God has claimed us as God's own children in baptism. With the outstretched embrace of the crucified Christ God has framed us at the center of divine love. When God raised Jesus from the grave we were filled with overwhelming joy. Now what? It would be so easy to go right back to the same-old-same-old reality. It would be easy to slip back into our almost-but-not-quite faithful enough lifestyle.

However, today the crowd's question becomes our question. Today, God's response becomes our answer. Pay careful attention here. Our text is not a handy dandy three step game plan for the crowds to follow in order to stop emotional pain. The text is not a guaranteed action plan for us to earn God's love. It is not a magic formula detailing how we can convert others to Jesus all by ourselves.

Remember, Peter has just described God's own well-planned acts of love in Jesus. God had taken the initiative then and is continuing to take charge of that saving action plan.

So, what are the crowds to do? Peter responds, "Save yourselves from this corrupt generation" (Acts 2:40). At first glance, it looks like God wants us all to save ourselves. However, a closer look at this phrase shows us that it can also be translated, "Let yourselves be saved." Aha! It is God who does the saving. It is God's people who let God act through them and for them. It is God's people whom Peter encourages to "let go" of their need to be in control of everything and "let God" show them what God has promised for them and for their children and "for everyone whom the Lord our God calls to him" (Acts 2:39).

Now is God's saving game plan coming into focus? It begins with what God has done, is doing, and promises to continue doing. It begins with God's saving claim of us and

God's loving frame around us. Because God is in charge, therefore, we can change. Because in Jesus God has turned the world's view of reality upside down, therefore, we are not trapped and entombed by old ways of thinking and feeling. Because God has turned toward us first, therefore it is possible now for us to turn toward God. Because God raised Jesus, we therefore can heed Peter's words and stick to the God's saving game plan: "Repent and be baptized every one of you in the name of Jesus" (Acts 2:38).

Repentance can be a difficult and scary concept for even the most faithful Christians to understand. In our culture, many who encounter the word imagine a screaming football coach, a pleading politician, or a pulpit pounding preacher. These folks are often portrayed by the media as standing in front of frightened people promising punishment and pain unless they respond with lasting behavior change. "Return to the straight and narrow or be trapped and skewered by Satan's harrow" was a familiar threat that echoed throughout upper Midwestern farm country during the nineteenth century.

That would cut to the heart all right! So, might simply and quietly recalling the guilt and shame of our own sin. Stirred up emotions can, indeed, motivate us to change our ways of thinking and behaving... to repent. However, remember that emotions fire up fast and soon fizzle away, most often resulting in no change whatsoever. We are just not able to change all by ourselves. That's impossible. Paul describes his own captivity to sin in these words:

> For I do not do the good I want, but the evil I do not want is what I do... wretched man I am! Who will rescue me from the body of death? Thanks be to God through Jesus Christ our Lord.
> — Romans 7:19, 24-25

Nevertheless, the Easter message is this: because God has done the impossible in Jesus, therefore, we receive the impossible through Jesus. Because Jesus broke the bonds of sin and death for us, we can also turn away from their control over us. "Repent" now has a new meaning because God is in charge. Christ is risen! He is risen indeed! Alleluia! Now we can, as Peter proclaims, let ourselves be saved from sin's captivity. We can let ourselves be changed, forgiven, splashed, and loved into a new community.

Pastor Terry was trying to figure out the best way to explain the meaning of "repent" to four- and five-year-old Sunday school students. Finally instead of using textbook words, she decided to use a show and tell demonstration. First, she instructed their teacher, Miss Jean, to stand in the far corner of the room. At Pastor Terry's signal, Miss Jean would start chanting "Let's do bad things! Let's do bad things!" The teacher's helper, Thomas, a ninth grader and cross bearer during worship, was to be Jesus. He was told to stand in the opposite corner holding the processional cross used in worship. At Pastor Terry's signal Thomas was to follow the children closely, stand in their midst, and say, "Jesus loves you, follow him," and walk back to his corner.

Then Pastor Terry gathered the young children in the corner of the room near Thomas. She told them to stay near Jesus and sing "Jesus Loves Me" until they heard Miss Jean's voice. Then they would leave Jesus and move toward Miss Jean. Then when they heard Pastor Terry say "repent" the children were to turn away from Miss Jean and start back toward Jesus. Well, you can imagine what the next few noisy minutes were like in that Sunday school classroom. Over and over the same pattern took place. Children gathered and sung at the cross. They heard sin's enticing voice and stopped singing. They left Jesus and walked toward "the bad things."

At the same time Jesus followed close behind. When the pastor shouted, "Repent," the children turned around and began to walk across the room. However, when they turned around, they discovered "Jesus" right there in the center. Back and forth went the children, turning way from Jesus who never turned away from them; who was always with them whenever they walked.

Thanks, Pastor Terry. Thanks children, for showing us what it means to repent... turn toward Jesus who has already turned toward us. Thanks for showing us that following Jesus is much more than being fired up with emotional highs or being fizzled out with emotional lows. Thanks for showing us that we can follow Jesus because Jesus has already:

claimed us as his own with a baptismal splash; framed us in the forgiving center of his love with a crucified embrace; changed us by breaking the power of sin and death with an Easter morning shout of resurrection. Christ is risen! He is risen indeed! Alleluia!

Amen.

Framed, Changed, Challenged

The week before classes began, Harold, a high school history teacher, fell off a step ladder and injured his back. For the next three months he was forced to wear a plaster cast around the entire upper part of his body. The cast fit so well underneath his shirt and sport coat that it was not at all noticeable.

On the first day of class, with the cast under his shirt, Harold discovered that he had been assigned the rowdiest and most rebellious students in the whole school. Walking confidently into his boisterous and disorderly classroom, Harold opened the windows and then busied himself at his desk until the bell rang to indicate the beginning of what looked like a very long history class. When a strong breeze started Harold's necktie flapping in his face, Harold calmly picked up his desk stapler and stapled the unruly tie to his chest. That little demonstration got everybody's attention. Harold had no discipline problems that semester. During the next few weeks, students began to look at Harold with new respect. Their grades improved, their attendance increased, and their number of detentions declined.

Soon other teachers and even the school principal began to notice the changes in Harold's students. One afternoon after students had gone home, some of Harold's peers asked him how he had accomplished the impossible. Harold replied, "Well, I just did something ridiculous and humiliating that got their attention." Then Harold described the tie stapling incident. Continuing on, Harold explained, "Well, you might have guessed that after a week or so, students began to realize that I was not a full-contact boxing champion and that I was actually wearing a cast. I was afraid that their old rowdy, disrespectful behavior would come back worse than ever. Fortunately, it did not. They had begun to appreciate the new respect from other teachers and students. Every day we challenged each other. It's surprising, but we actually seem to like each other... most of the time anyway."

Hmmm... something ridiculous, humiliating, and impossible that changes everything. Sounds a lot like the crucified and risen Jesus, doesn't it? On the cross Jesus framed us in the center of his love. Through his resurrection Jesus changed us from a people with little meaning and purpose into a new fellowship with mission and focus.

Today's text describes what that new fellowship in Christ looked like then. As we explore this lesson, listen for the spirit's challenge to faithful living today. Pay careful attention to the results too. Notice how the behavior of these first Christians got the attention of others. Here is an excellent "show-and-tell" model of Christian witness.

So what were the basic characteristics of that early Christian community? Look at the first verse: "They devoted themselves to the apostles' teaching and fellowship, to the breaking of bread and the prayers" (Acts 2:42).

First, it was crucial for those early Christians to know the story of Jesus as told by the eyewitnesses, the apostles themselves. Here Christians learned how their experience of Jesus as Messiah was described in their own scripture. Here they discovered what it really meant to be named as Christ's followers, claimed by Christ himself, and framed in Christ's own embrace. Here they began to grasp a vision of what Christ was challenging them to be and to do.

Second, living in close and daily fellowship with other Christians was essential. It was within this fellowship that many astonishing "wonders and signs were being done by the apostles" (Acts 2:43). It was within this fellowship that encouragement was given, faith matured, friendships grew, and even material needs were addressed with generosity (Acts 2:44, 35). Something unusual, substantial, and unique was happening within this new community.

Third, these first church members gathered to break bread; sharing meals at home (literally, the Greek here is translated "from house to house") nearly every day. Eating together in homes groomed and deepened relationships. Breaking bread together also broke down barriers that separated and inhibited relationships. Giving thanks and breaking bread together also connected the community with the risen Christ within a common and holy meal.

Fourth, these first Christians in Jerusalem remained faithful. They still worshiped regularly in the temple and maintained daily Jewish prayer routines (Acts 2:46).

So, what is the challenge that the risen Jesus lays before his changed people... you and me... the church? Well, when our text was written, the Spirit formed the church as an alternative community within Jewish society. Today, the Spirit of the risen Christ continues to form us as an alternative fellowship within our society. Although our languages differ, our cultures vary, our ethnicities diverge, and our politics are often diffuse, the shape of Christ's community looks very much the same as that described in today's scripture lesson. 1) Know the Jesus story; 2) Live daily within the fellowship of encouraging, supporting, and serving people; 3) Share meals together often in one another's homes; 4) Worship and pray together regularly.

Now, here comes a refreshing surprise especially for those who are worried about declining church membership and a reduced Christian influence in modern society. Notice the attitudes and behavior of those early Christians as they went about their daily lives "with glad and generous hearts praising God and having the goodwill of all the people"

(Acts 2:46-47). Now, notice what happened next. "Day by day the Lord added to their number" (Acts 2:47).

It was the attitudes and behavior of these Christians that God used to get the respect and goodwill of the people. It wasn't three-step strategies or free camel rides. It wasn't fancy greeter badges or even changes in worship style that did it. Folks simply saw behaviors change, generosity flow, and attitudes improve. Then the Lord (not a committee) drew them into this growing community of changed people. Then, together they learned the Jesus story, shared the fellowship, broke some bread, and prayed together. That same challenge is ours today.

Here is just one actual example of what that faithfulness looks like. Some of you may have heard about this.

It happened a few years ago at a high school football game between the Lions and the Tornadoes. The Lions belonged to a Christian school with supportive and involved parents, up-to-date equipment, and a 7-1 record. The Tornadoes were from a state juvenile correctional facility. Many of the players had convictions for drugs and assault. Many had been disowned by their families. Their equipment was old and worn. Their record was 0-8.

Kris, the head coach of the Lions, decided that this game was an opportunity to show what the love of Jesus might look like. He sent letters and emails to Lion parents and fans asking for volunteers to cheer for the Tornadoes. In his message, Kris said, "Imagine if you don't have a home life; if everyone had given up on you. Now imagine what it would mean if hundreds of people believed in you and even cheered for you by name."

At game time, the Tornadoes took the field running through a 40-yard double line of screaming fans and cheerleaders yelling, "Go, Tornadoes!" During the game Tornado players heard hundreds of fans behind their team bench cheering for them by their first names.

When both teams gathered on the fifty-yard line for the customary post-game prayer, one of the Tornadoes players asked to lead. Coach Kris still remembers it word for word: "Lord I don't know how this happened and I don't know how to say thank you. I would never have thought there were so many people in this world who cared about us."

As the Tornadoes got back on their bus, they were each handed a bag containing a fast food meal, a Bible, and a letter of encouragement from one of the Lion players. Before the bus left, the tornado coach hugged Coach Kris, thanked him and said, "You'll never be able to know what your folks did for these kids tonight. Thank you."

But who won the game? Jesus of course. He has framed, changed, and challenged us to show the same compassion to others.

What signs of wonder and encouragement are part of everyday life in your congregation? What generosity flows from your worship space into the world around you? How do you learn and teach the Jesus story? What does breaking bread from house to house look like for you? What about regular worship and prayer patterns? Where are the glad and generous hearts? Where is the goodwill of all the people outside the parish community?

These are challenging questions all right. Their answers can be downright depressing and humiliating if we try to answer them without Jesus. You see, it is Jesus who gets our attention with his brutal, ridiculous, humiliating death on the cross. It is Jesus who frames us in his outstretched arms. It is Jesus who changes the way we view the world's reality with his resurrection from the grave. It is Jesus who challenges us to live so faithfully that others are drawn into new life. It is Jesus who makes the impossible possible. Christ is risen! He is risen indeed! Alleluia! Amen.

Easter 5
Acts 7:55-60

Looking for Ducklings:
Kissing the Sidewalk

Poor Daryl. One moment he was enjoying a beautiful springtime walk looking for ducklings along a lakeside nature trail. The next moment he was lying face down on the sidewalk, wondering where all the blood came from. As he was struggling to his feet a park ranger rushed over with a towel and first aid kit. After cleaning blood from Daryl's face and making sure that Daryl was not seriously injured, the ranger said, "I noticed that when you tripped you were looking out at the lake instead of at the path. What were you looking for anyway?" When Daryl told him, the ranger replied, "Well, sir, there are baby ducks all over the place this time of year. You can't miss them. From now on, keep at least one eye on the sidewalk before you get another close up view." (Daryl was okay. The only injury was to his pride.)

Without realizing it, the ranger asked a very important Easter season question for all of us. "What are you looking for anyway?" Jesus asked Mary Magdalene almost the same thing on that very first Easter morning: "Whom are you looking for?" (John 20:15). Now, remember this well: What you are looking for can determine what you see and do not see. Whom you are looking for can determine whom you see and do not see.

Before sunrise on that first Easter morning Mary Magdalene came to Jesus' tomb looking for and expecting to find the body of Jesus. When she saw only an empty tomb she ran to Simon Peter and John and told them the "facts" as she "saw" them; even adding something. Instead of simply

95

saying that Jesus' body wasn't in the tomb anymore, Mary concluded that an unknown "they" had done this. So, who knows what Simon Peter and John might have been thinking as they raced back to the tomb. Who could have done this? The Romans? The high priest's soldiers? Some misguided group of followers? What were they looking for? Whom were they looking for... even after they found the empty tomb and the rolled up grave cloth and wrappings? Mary Magdalene stayed behind, looking into the tomb and crying. What was she looking for? A dead body and not a living Lord would be a good guess. She said as much to the two angels whom she actually saw sitting on the very place where Jesus' body had been earlier.

What you are looking for really does shape what you actually see and do not see even if it's right there in front of your face. Remember Daryl, the ducklings, and the sidewalk? Whom you are looking for really does shape whom you actually expect to see and whom you do not expect to see, even if she or he is right there in front of you.

Left alone to cope with her grief, Mary may have seen only a stranger whom she thought was the gardener (John 20:15). Instead of this Easter question from the risen Christ, Mary might have heard only a "May I help you?" question from a cemetery gardener.

It was the living Lord himself who opened Mary's eyes and heart to see that he was the answer to this Easter question. It is the living Lord himself who opens our eyes and hearts to see that he alone answers our questions this Fifth Sunday of Easter. What are you looking for? Whom are you looking for? Here, in the community of the risen Christ, is the living Lord who sees deep into your soul and still accepts you, who know the powerful hungers of your heart and still loves you, and who understands the guilt of things you have done and left undone and still offers you forgiveness.

Today, the Fifth Sunday of Easter, our scripture lesson proclaims still another powerful response to the Easter question. Today the Spirit shows us the risen Jesus as "the Son of Man standing at the right hand of God" (Acts 7:56). Today, we are looking for one who is really in charge beyond the influence of the troubles and confusion of the world. Today the Spirit shows us the exalted Jesus, the Son of Main, reigning with God. Today the Spirit shows us that the kingdom of God and of his Christ has already begun. Today, the risen Christ again welcomes us into it.

Our daily lives can spin out of control in an instant. (Remember Daryl and the sidewalk?) Sometimes it seems like it takes all of our efforts and energy simply to avoid a total collapse into chaos. Here in this community, the risen Christ, the Son of Man, reminds us that he is in charge. We are not and will never be. Here in this community, the Spirit of God who created the universe out of chaos, gives us a vision of the one who brings order in the midst of confusion, courage in the midst of cowardice, and calm in the midst of life's storms. Today our text gives us a vision of the Son of Man who is in control when our lives spiral out of control.

It was this claim that Jesus is standing with God as the Son of Man that finally got Stephen killed, you know. Stephen was one of a group of seven who were chosen to assist with distributing food to poor families in the community. After the resurrection, the Word of God spread quickly in Jerusalem and even many Jewish priests became part of the community (Acts 6:1-7). Finally members of one synagogue were fed up, particularly with Stephen's ability not only to perform wondrous deeds, but also to speak with persuasive power. So, they stirred up their own members as well as the Jewish council who were compelled to bring Stephen in for a hearing before them (Acts 6:8-15).

The first 53 verses of chapter 7 are filled with Stephen's fiery "trash talk" at the hearings. He attacked the very history and identity that the Jews had worked so hard to maintain during Roman occupation. He not only insulted his Jewish contemporaries, he also insulted their ancestors. He called them all stiff-necked people with uncircumcised hearts. They had sold Joseph into slavery, rejected Moses, turned to idols, persecuted prophets, broken God's law, murdered Jesus, and opposed the Holy Spirit (Acts 7:1-53). Wow!

How would you feel if someone publicly insulted your ancestors, your history, and your values… literally everything that gave meaning to your life? What would you do? Probably react with outbursts of rage, which is what the Jewish leaders did (Acts 7:54). Yet they did not seek to kill Stephen at first. In fact, by Roman law, Jewish courts could not sentence anyone to death. The council members were filled with rage. Stephen was filled with the Holy Spirit.

Here is what changed the leaders from an enraged council to a lynch mob. It was all about power and control. When Stephen proclaimed that he saw the risen Jesus, standing at the right hand of God, this was the last straw. Trash talking was one thing. Even claiming that Jesus was resurrected was not enough to drive them over the edge. However, when Stephen declared that Jesus was standing with God as Son of Man, exalted Lord and Messiah, then that was it. They had heard enough. They went out of control over the very issue of control.

With a loud shout, they rushed Stephen and dragged him out to kill him… trying to regain some order in the midst of chaos; trying to show each other that they had not lost control. Stephen and his contemptible vision was dead. Their stones put a stop to that blasphemy forever. Or so they thought. The Son of Man still reigned. They were not in charge of this kingdom anymore. God would use one of their own, an eyewitness named Saul (Acts 7:58), to show the world who was really in control.

So, back to our Easter question: What are you looking for? Whom are you looking for? Today's Easter answers are not about why we should be ready to be martyrs. They are not about Stephen either. Today's Easter answers are less about martyrdom and more about a message of good news and the reign of the Son of Man.

God used the message of Stephen's vision to build a new community with a new reality within a new kingdom. The new kingdom is not about the control of princes, priests, or kings. It is about the power of the risen and reigning Christ, the Son of Man himself.

Because God revealed this to Stephen, Stephen was able to suffer and even to die with the courage and confidence of Christ's continuing presence with him. While the stones were flying, Stephen could still pray, "Lord Jesus receive my spirit" (Acts 7:59). Here was not only the bedtime prayer of Jewish children (see Psalm 31:15) it also echoed Jesus' own prayer on the cross (Luke 23:46).

Today God also welcomes us into this new community where the Son of Man reigns, in control. Here the risen Jesus gives us himself in bread and wine and word. Here within God's people gathered, the risen Christ gives us the confidence and courage to face the troubles and struggles of our lives.

Because God gave Stephen a vision of the risen Christ standing at God's right hand Stephen could use Christ's own prayer to ask God to forgive the sins of his murderers (Acts 7:60 and Luke 23:34). Because God shows us what forgiveness looks like in the baptismal waters and in the promise of the risen Christ, we can also forgive others.

What are you looking for today? Whom are you looking for? Remember Daryl, the fellow who started out looking for baby ducks and ended up falling face first on the sidewalk? Two days later he was scheduled to serve as a communion assistant for the first time. Poor Daryl. All he could think of was his swollen lip, his bruised cheeks, and his black eye. What an ugly mess! Why did he volunteer to serve at the Lord's Table this week anyway? What if he offered the wine, speaking the words "this is the blood of Christ shed for you" and then, one by one, people would see his face and reply, "none for me thanks" or "I'll pass on that today"? That would be so embarrassing he might have to join another parish. Everybody would laugh at him, or think he'd been in a fight, or even had been falling down drunk. Similar thoughts raced through Daryl's mind as the worship service progressed that Sunday. And then Daryl heard Pastor Richard preaching to the congregation: "Life is not all about you. It's not all about us. It is not all about what we look like or what we sound like. It's all about Jesus. Always. You are not in control. It is Jesus."

"Oh yeah, I remember now," thought Daryl to himself and began to serve Jesus to his sisters and brothers in Christ. Oh, yes, nobody passed on the gift.

What are you looking for today? Whom are you looking for? Do not worry if you aren't really certain of anything except the empty space deep inside yourself. Don't be discouraged if you find it hard to find your way through confusing and troubled times. Don't be disappointed if it's still hard to find control in your life right now. The good news is that God has already found you and welcomes you into a new reality where God is always present. The risen Christ gives you courage to continue, and the Son of Man reigns with God forever. Christ is risen! He is risen indeed! Alleluia! Amen.

Stuck in Park

Martha had lived alone for several years, except, that is, for her dog, Otto, a three-year-old miniature shi-tsu. Martha and Otto went everywhere together. Even where dogs were not permitted, Otto was content to wait patiently in the car for Martha to return. One particular sunny afternoon Martha had to make a quick stop at the corner grocery store. As was her custom, Martha rolled down the windows to make sure the inside of the car would be comfortable. Otto curled up on the backseat, and Martha started toward the store. Worrying that her dog might jump out of the car window, Martha stopped every few steps, pointed at her car, and commanded "Otto! You stay!"

A young man carrying a skateboard observed Martha's actions in silence. Finally he just had to ask, "Ma'am, why don't you just put it in park?"

Our young friend didn't see the whole picture. He was totally oblivious to the dog on the backseat. His point of view of the situation was certainly different than Martha's.

Unfortunately, when it comes to sharing God's good news in Jesus, many of us Christians only see a small part of the picture. We ignore the context of those whom we are trying to reach. Many of us tend to see strangers as consumers and customers who must be persuaded to "purchase" our spiritual "products." If we could just learn the current techniques and use the right words, well, more folks would sign up. Then we could meet our budget and have better programs. On the other hand, many folks are reluctant to even visit a congregation, fearing that they will become manipulated objects of the latest member recruiting sales pitch: "What will it take for you to join the church/tithe your income/chair a committee today?"

Too few of us take time to see the whole picture — "The shi-tsu on the seat" — as we go about our daily lives. Many of us are too quick to "leave it in park." We are not quite satisfied with the way things are, but not really motivated enough to look at possibilities. It's too easy to put visitors on a new list of "prospective buyers" rather than to welcome them as guests in a new community. It's too easy to see them as potential contributors rather than to greet them with dignity as children of God. It's too easy to focus on their possible future membership with us rather than to honor God's current and promised relationship with them.

Our first lesson today opens our eyes to see what sharing God's good news in Jesus can look like. First, Paul walks the walk, as Jesus did. Second, Paul honors relationships, as Jesus did. Finally, Paul shares the good news, as Jesus was, is, and will always be.

In Jesus, God's own self became flesh and lived among God's people (John 1:14). Jesus did not use his carpentry skills to build some sort of shrine near his Nazareth home and then use high pressure gimmicks to get folks to join up. Instead, Jesus, walked among God's people: priests and commoners, Pharisees and prostitutes, lepers and leaders, Roman soldiers and Jewish rebels, sick and healthy, Jews and Gentiles, outcasts and in-groups. Jesus walked the walk in the midst of all God's children.

This is exactly what Paul was doing. Just before this lesson begins, we find Paul walking around Athens for a few days, waiting to be joined by Silas and Timothy, his missionary partners (Acts 17:15-16). Athens was located halfway between Rome, the center of imperial power, and Jerusalem, the center of the growing Christian community. Although

Athens was part of the vast Roman Empire, it was still a focal point for Greek religion, philosophy, and culture. Tourists from all over the Roman Empire flocked here to see the places where the famous philosophers Socrates, Plato, Epicurus, and Zeno had taught. They visited the famous Parthenon dedicated to the goddess Athena. They wandered past many other religious sites containing idols that represented many different gods and goddesses.

During his walks Paul dropped in at Jewish synagogues. Every day he wandered through the civic center market place and talked with whomever happened to be there (Acts 17:17). He engaged in discussions with well educated and arrogant Stoic and Epicurean philosophers. He even experienced their ridicule. One of the insults from a learned philosopher was to accuse a student of having no depth of thought whatsoever. These scholars called Paul a "babbler" literally translated as "retailer of scraps" (Acts 17:18). Today we might use the terms "bumper sticker faith" or "cut-and-paste" theologian; one who strings together a lot of shallow catch phrases and half-truths.

Paul walked the walk all right. He didn't require or even expect people to come to him. He wandered among them. He didn't use gimmicks to induce folks to become church members. He listened to their ideas, endured their insults, and continued to "tell the good news about Jesus and the resurrection" (Acts 17:18).

What would happen if you walked the walk around the communities and neighborhoods where your congregation is located? What if you made this journey as if you were a first time visitor like Paul? What might you see and hear... really? What if you attended worship in your congregation as if you were there for the first time? What might good news look like here? How might you share it?

Paul's wandering around, walking the walk around Athens, resulted in an invitation to address members of the council of Athens, called the Areopagus. It was this group of leading scholars who controlled the right to lecture on religious issues within the city of Athens. Before the Roman conquest, this was a very influential court. It was located on The Hill of Ares, the Greek god of war (re-named Mars Hill, for the Roman war god). Later during Paul's time, this group met in the city, interestingly enough, in the Hall of Zeus, the supreme god of ancient Greece. So, here was Paul, a Christian invited into a religious discussion by a bunch of Greek philosophers inside a building named for a pagan god (Acts 17:19 and 20).

Today's text begins with Paul honoring relationships and giving dignity and respect to the worldviews of his hearers. Here, as did Jesus, Paul met people where they were, rather than where he thought they should be. Here Paul worked to build relationships rather than to diminish them. Here Paul acknowledged their own ways of finding meaning in life through religion and philosophy (Acts 17:22-23). He even quoted one of their own poets (Acts 17:29). Notice that Paul sought common ground in a common humanity within a common creation. Paul heard their own searching and yearning for God and affirmed it also as his own. He invited them to consider that "this very God is not far from each one of us" (Acts 17:27).

Paul honors relationships by meeting people where they are, listening to how they define reality, speaking in terms that both can understand... without taking offence. In our text, Paul is meeting with Gentiles, not Jews. Notice that Paul does not describe the sinful and fallen nature of humanity and the wrath of God. Notice that Paul doesn't quote scripture to folks who don't know or accept scripture. Paul does not discuss Jewish law and prophets as he would have if he were in a synagogue. Once again, remember, Paul is in a Gentile city, speaking with scholars of Gentile philosophy and religion, and meeting within a building named after a powerful Gentile god. Paul does not denounce the Athenian's identity and meaning. Instead he praises their religiosity and searching.

As you walk around your community, you will meet many who are also searching for meaning and purpose in life. You will meet many folks who share the same heart hungers that you have. How will you meet them where they are? How will you, like Paul, listen first to understand their reality before even attempting to impose your own views? How will you, like Paul, strive to honor your mutual relationship through the creator before inviting them to share your own relationship with Christ in the Christian community?

Here's an interesting story. Perhaps you have heard it before. A seminary professor was walking alongside a fast flowing stream. As he was looking for a place to cross safely, he noticed a faculty colleague walking along the opposite shoreline. "Hey, how did you get to the other side?" he shouted.

"You are on the other side," his friend replied. Hmmm…

You see, this is often what happens when we fail to meet folks where they are, respecting their views and listening to their yearnings. This is what happens when we fail to understand that from where they are standing, we are on the other side. This is what happens when we treat folks only as consumers and customers to be persuaded to purchase our product and join our congregation.

The good news here is that Paul's address before the Greek council actually is a show-and-tell demonstration of what it looks like to be in relationship with each other and in so doing, be in relationship with God the creator. For Paul, there is really no way to convince folks to join the "other side." Instead there is an invitation to discover the "something more," that God shares with "all sides."

Now, finally, in our text Paul shares the good news... the "something more" that the council had heard about and invited him to explain to them. This something more is a call to think "outside the box" about meaning and purpose in life. Coloring inside the lines drawn by Greek philosophy and religion wasn't enough anymore. Paul says it this way:

> *While God had overlooked the times of human ignorance, now*
> *he commands all people everywhere to repent.*
>
> — Acts 17:30

Repent is God's invitation to turn toward something more, or for Paul, toward someone more... the risen Jesus Christ. Through the resurrection of Jesus, God has already "acted outside the box" and "colored outside the lines." God had turned toward them first, deepening a relationship of love.

God's Easter good news here is that in the risen Christ there is no "other side." There is only God's embrace on every side. God's good news welcomes us into a "something more" community with a splash of baptismal water. Here the risen Christ strengthens us for our daily journey with a taste of bread broken and wine poured. Here God's good news in Christ takes our timid hearts out of park and sends us out to walk the walk, to build relationships, and to invite folks into God's something more. Amen.

Stargazing, Naval Gazing, and Other Waiting Games

Hurry up and wait! Hurry up and wait! Anyone who has spent time in the military has heard this and lived this as a part of their daily routine. Rapid flurries of activity are followed by long periods of waiting in line. Waiting seems to be part of life in every context. We wait in lines at grocery stores, department stores, banks, athletic events, concerts, motor vehicle offices, and government agencies. It seems like time passes with the speed of light on our way there and at the pace of a slug after we finally arrive. Much of our daily lives seems to be spent waiting — for traffic jams to clear, mail to arrive, workweeks to end, sermons to conclude, the weather to change.

So, what do you do while you are waiting? Some folks fuss and fume, staring at their watches impatiently. Some bring something to read. Some worry about anything and everything. Others do absolutely noting at all. What is waiting like for you? What is it like when you are unable to control the unexpected and unwanted delays in your busy life? What goes through your mind when you discover that you are powerless to restore order in a confusing and scary situation?

These are the two essential Ascension Day questions that our text addresses. In the first, the apostles ask Jesus, "Lord, is this the time when you restore the kingdom to Israel?" (Acts 1:6). In the next, two angels ask the apostles, "Men of Galilee, why do you stand looking up toward heaven?" (Acts 1:11).

Now remember, each of these questions emerged from the apostles' own anxiety. They had no idea what might happen next. The future was uncertain at best. Even the immediate present was beyond their control. Reality as they knew it had ended. Something new was happening all right. Jesus — the one who was crucified and buried and now resurrected? Yeah, that Jesus — had been speaking with them about the kingdom of God for about forty days now. He told them to hang around Jerusalem and wait there to be baptized with the Holy Spirit (Acts 1:3-5). What would this new kingdom be like? Would the occupying Romans be kicked out of Judea? Would those uppity Pharisees and priests finally get a reality check? Would Jesus ask the apostles to be in charge of things? Just when would Jesus start the restoration ball rolling? It would be easier to prepare for all this if only Jesus would at least give them a target date.

Star gazing and naval gazing, drifting and dreaming in their private reality, the apostles did not quite get it yet. The new kingdom wasn't all about them. It wasn't all about their wants and needs. It wasn't all about gaining control over a world that seems to be in chaos. It wasn't all about getting secret insider knowledge of exactly how long they would have to wait for the followers of Jesus to be in control.

In fact, Jesus said as much to the apostles when he replied, "It is not for you to know the times or periods that the Father has set by his own authority" (Acts 1:7). God is in charge of God's kingdom. The apostles were not. We are not.

Of course, waiting is hard. It's scary and frustrating. It's aggravating and confusing. It's difficult enough when you don't know when it will be over. However, when you are given an impossible task to accomplish while you wait, it's downright overwhelming.

Have you noticed that not only did Jesus refuse to give details about the kingdom of God, he also told the apostles not even to ask when it would appear. Then he told them they would receive some power soon when the Holy Spirit came upon them. Power to do what? The Spirit would give them power to witness while they wait… power to be Jesus' "witnesses in Jerusalem, in all Judea and Samaria, and to the ends of the earth" (Acts 1:8). Huh?

Impossible and overwhelming for sure. How were they to do this anyway? Was Jesus going to stay with them and instruct them in what to say and how to say it and when and where to say it? Jerusalem would be difficult enough but to walk all over Judea and Samaria would take years. Going to the ends of the earth or even around the whole Roman Empire was just plain ridiculous. Never happen. Couldn't happen.

Then Jesus got the apostles' attention again with another demonstration that he was in charge and they were not. Now Jesus was about to show them that they were partially correct; they would not be able to accomplish this mission all by themselves even if Jesus in his resurrected body went with them. Jesus would see that they would have power to undertake the impossible. This power would proceed from Jesus himself when the Holy Spirit came upon them.

Confusing? Yes. Overwhelming? Of course. Did the apostles' mission still seem impossible? Certainly.

Immediately after Jesus told the apostles that they would be his witness to the ends of the earth our text states: "As they were watching, he was lifted up, and a cloud took him from their sight" (Acts 1:9). That got their attention all right. Jesus' resurrection appearances were over. The reign of the exalted Christ had begun. A new community, the church, was about to take shape. The apostles were about to find out that the ascended Lord was not a past Lord; but an always present and contemporary Christ. Somehow, Jesus would show them this. Somehow the ascended Lord would bring order in their confusion. Somehow, as he always did, Jesus would show them who was, is, and would always be in control in the midst of chaos.

Here's a story that you may not have heard before. Pastor Kathy enjoyed visiting in parishioner's homes and work places. One afternoon, Barbara invited Pastor Kathy to ride along as she made a regular delivery from her pet store. Every half mile or so, Barbara would stop the van, get out, pick up a two by four from behind the driver's seat, and whack the side of the van. Then she would drive down the road again. After seeing Barbara repeat this process a few times, Pastor Kathy's curiosity got the best of her. "Why in the world are you doing this over and over?" She asked Barbara. "Is there something wrong with your van?"

"Nope," replied Barbara? "It's the best one-ton van I ever had."

"Well then, why do you keep whacking it with that two-by-four?" wondered her pastor.

"You see pastor, today I have two tons of parakeets in back. Every so often I have to whack the side and get their attention so that half of them fly in the air. After a half mile or so they start to settle down, so I whack the van again," Barbara answered.

Jesus got the apostles' attention with many show-and-tell demonstrations from feeding and healing to dying and rising. Each time their zeal diminished and their energy dissipated Jesus got them moving back again to the center of mission.

The apostles were ready to enjoy the physical presence of the risen Jesus forever. Those past forty days of advanced instruction at the feet of Jesus was great. They had become a tight little band of Jesus people. Perhaps soon Jesus would give them the secret of world conquest and establish the kingdom of God forever. It didn't really matter exactly when that would happen. Jesus could keep that to himself if he wanted. Soon they would show those know-it-all Pharisees whom God really likes. Soon they'd show those Romans a thing or two about military operations.

Well, their one pound brains were filling up with two pounds of hot air. Here they were, gathered just outside Jerusalem on the Mount of Olives exactly where God's kingdom would begin. Maybe Jesus was about to commission them as heavenly warriors in the new kingdom. Then Jesus told them that they were not to be warriors for an earthly kingdom, but to be witnesses to a new king and a transformed reality. Hmmm, that got the apostles' attention.

Before they could ask Jesus for more information, or at least some clarification... whoosh!... Jesus ascended into heaven. That got their attention too, but it didn't get them moving. Instead they stood in stunned silence, gazing toward heaven. Now what? Then two angels appeared, not with a two by four, but with a question that would get them focused and moving forward. "Men of Galilee, why do you stand looking up toward heaven?" (Acts 1:11). It's time to get busy. Stop star gazing and naval gazing. It's time to get busy.

Jesus left the apostles with a specific promise of power from the Holy Spirit and a precise mission to witness for Jesus to the ends of the earth. Jesus gives us the same promise and the same mission.

How does the Lord get your attention? How does the Lord move you from feeling religious emotions to doing faithful deeds? What do you do when you find yourselves waiting around for specific directions and they never seem to come?

Celebrating the Ascension of Our Lord is really celebrating who really is in charge of a new reality and acknowledging who is not. Celebrating the Ascension of our Lord is celebrating the reign of Christ who has broken the controlling bonds of all earthly kingdoms. Because of Christ's ascension, the kingdom of God is not just out there somewhere

— the kingdom of God is within the people gathered, within this bread broken, and this wine poured. The kingdom of God is within the water splashed and the word proclaimed.

Here, as we celebrate ascension, the Lord Christ gets our attention and moves us forward with a mission in his name. Amen.

Lesson from a Chipmunk

In today's first lesson the apostles are gathered with their families in an upstairs room somewhere in Jerusalem. So much had happened during the past few months that it was hard to put it all together. They had accompanied Jesus into the city, receiving a royal welcome fit for a king. Then there was their last supper together, followed by Judas' betrayal and the arrest in Gethsemane, their own narrow escape from the soldiers, and that most horrible crucifixion. They had just about given up all hope when the risen Jesus appeared before them, ate with them, and then for six more weeks instructed them about the kingdom of God. Just when it all started to make sense, just when Jesus gave them a promise and a purpose, he left them again. This time they saw it for themselves. Immediately after Jesus promised them that the Holy Spirit would give them power to be witnesses through- out the world (Acts 1:8), "He was lifted up, and a cloud took him out of their sight" (Acts 1:9).

Now what were they to think? When were they going to get this power? What were they supposed to do until then? And when the Holy Spirit did give them power (of course Je- sus didn't even tell them when that might be, let alone when God would bring in the new kingdom), how is that going to help them witness to the very ends of the earth? Those earli- est Christians must have been overwhelmed and confused trying to adjust to one life-changing experience after anther. What could they count on? Whom could they depend upon? Many questions. Few answers. Just a promise and a purpose, a gift and a mission.

How do you adjust to all the rapid changes in today's society? How does your congregation respond to changes within the community? Changes within yourselves? How do you respond when you are overwhelmed and confused by changes happening all around you? What can you count on when everything seems to be out of control? Whom can you depend on, really?

Pastor Tom was getting into his car in the church parking lot one afternoon when he noticed a tiny chipmunk nestled comfortably in the shadows just behind the driver's side front tire. This effectively stopped the pastor from backing out of his parking space. Unable to back up and unwilling to drive across the church lawn, Pastor Tom began clapping his hands loudly, attempting to encourage the chipmunk to move! This tactic worked immediately. The startled chipmunk darted away. Unfortunately, it settled behind the front tire on the passenger side. Again Pastor Tom clapped. This time our chipmunk ran to the right rear tire. By now you have already guessed that two more clapping episodes, accompanied by some yelling as well as a gathering audience of neighborhood children brought our little furry friend back to its original spot. Suddenly, Pastor Tom, the children, and especially the chipmunk heard loud and insistent chattering from a larger chipmunk sitting beneath the grape vines bordering the lawn. Hearing a welcome voice and seeing a familiar face, our little friend scooted off to safety.

Perhaps the chipmunk regaled his family and friends with stories of the many fast and scary changes he had experienced. Perhaps he chattered his thank yous to them repeatedly. Who knows, he may have gained a new appreciation for what really matters in life; for what you really need to hold onto when changes are happening all around you.

Here's a lesson for all of us. When the challenges of life become overwhelming, stay close to where you know the love is. Our chipmunk friend never strayed from where he

114

could see and hear the creature who loved him. No matter how large the threat or how terrifying the sounds, the chipmunk stayed close to the sure and certain sights and sounds of love. The sounds of promise soon became a visible reality as the frightened animal scampered from tire to tire, always staying close to the chatter of encouragement and the visibility of supportive relationships.

Here is the core of today's text. Here the risen Christ gives the overwhelmed apostles a promise and a purpose, a gift and a mission. Here in his parting words, Jesus promises them that the Holy Spirit will soon give them power for an amazing mission. In Jesus' own words, after receiving this gift, the apostles' purpose was to "… be my witnesses in Jerusalem, in all Judea and Samaria, and to the ends of the earth" (Acts 1:8). Incredible promise! Impossible purpose!

Just how were they going to accomplish all this? Where could they start? Who could they recruit to help them? What was their strategic plan? Where would their funding come from? What were the most critical scripture texts and theological insights necessary to implement this mission?

Before they could ask these questions, or even think of more, Jesus ascended into heaven. What an awesome sight that must have been! So, now what? Just stay here looking at the sky while they wait for the gift of power Jesus promised? Maybe Jesus would come back down soon, descending as the Son of Man to do battle for Jerusalem. Maybe these are the last days that the prophet Zechariah wrote about. This was the Mount of Olivet, after all, where all this was supposed to happen! (see Zechariah ch. 14).

While the apostles were staring at the clouds, suddenly two angels interrupted their silent musing. "Men of Galilee, why do you stand looking up at heaven? This Jesus… will come in the same way as you saw him go into heaven" (Acts 1:11). Doesn't this sound a lot like the two angels questions to the women visiting Jesus' tomb early Easter morning,

"Why do you look for the living among the dead?" He is not here, but has risen" (Luke 24:5). In other words, "Get busy. He gave you a mission to be his witnesses. So, get moving already."

Well, when the women first shared the angel's proclamation with the apostles, Luke states that "these words seemed to them an idle tale, and they did not believe them" (Luke 24:11). At least until they could verify the angels' message for themselves, that is. The risen Jesus appeared to them many times over the next forty days, eating with them and instructing them about the kingdom of God (Luke 24:12; Acts 1:6).

So, this time when the apostles saw (the same?) two angels for themselves, they believed them and got moving. They heard the promise of Jesus. They had a purpose to fulfill for Jesus. Now what they needed was to wait for the gift of power that would proceed from the ascended Jesus. How did the apostles cope with uncertainty and confusion as they waited for the promised gift? How did they begin to develop specific methods to address the overall purpose of their witness mission?

Today's text describes the apostles' response as well as some possibilities for ourselves. After all, the Lord has given us the same promise and purpose, the same gift and mission. It is likely that we, like the apostles, find ourselves waiting for more specific directions.

Where did they go? What did they do? They went where Jesus told them to go, Jerusalem (Acts 1:14, 12). Jerusalem and its immediate context was the foundational center of the Jewish religion. It was also the focal point of the mission of the church. Here is where the church began. From here is where Christianity spread. For the apostles, Jerusalem was the very center of God's loving actions; the intersection of promise and purpose, gift and mission. So the apostles walked back to Jerusalem, about one half mile from Mount Olivet.

Where do you go when you are anxious and confused by life challenges? The risen Jesus told the disciples to stay in Jerusalem. The ascended Jesus invites us to the center of God's loving actions for us and for the world. For us, that is the body of Christ, the church. Here is where we know the promise is heard and the gift of power is given. Here is where our mission is articulated and our specific purpose in life is clarified.

So, what did the apostles actually do when they got back to Jerusalem? What are we really supposed to do within the church? How does a general promise become a specific purpose? What is this gift and, how long do we have to wait before we get it?

Back in the city, the apostles remained close to where they knew God's love and encouragement were located — among God's faithful people. Our text names them specifically, including several women in addition to Jesus' own mother and brothers (Acts 1:13-14). While they waited, these early followers of Jesus "were constantly devoting themselves to prayer" (Acts 1:14). They didn't have to wait long before they received the gift of the Holy Spirit and their mission began. Jesus told them it would be "not many days from now" (Acts 1:5). Most Christians celebrate that festival day as Pentecost, or fifty days after Easter and forty days after Jesus' ascension (Acts 1:3).

God has already given us the gift that Jesus promised to the apostles. With a splash of baptismal water and a word of promise the Holy Spirit welcomes us into the Body of Christ, the fellowship where God's active love is demonstrated. Within this community, God's promise of forgiveness is boldly proclaimed and the risen and ascended Christ is shared. Constantly living and praying within this community of believers, God's people do receive guidance for growth and purpose for living.

Hang in there. Learn from the chipmunk. Stay close to where God shows you the love is... at the cross, an empty tomb, a splash of water, some bread broken, and some wine poured. Listen for God's word of love and forgiveness. Watch for the Spirit showing you what love looks like and sounds like in your own life.

Today, the ascended Christ has given you a promise of love and a gift of his presence. Open your hearts to receive it. Within that gift is a mission and a purpose. Pray with one another for understanding as you begin to unwrap it. Amen.